1st EDITION

Perspectives on Diseases and Disorders

Obesity

Other books is this series:

AIDS
Autism
Cancer
Diabetes
Eating Disorders

1st EDITION

Perspectives on Diseases and Disorders

Obesity

Tom and Gena Metcalf
Editors

Detroit • New York • San Francisco • New Haven, Conn. • Waterville, Maine • London

© 2008 Thomson Gale, a part of The Thomson Corporation.

Thomson and Star Logo are trademarks and Gale and Greenhaven Press are registered trademarks used herein under license.

For more information, contact:
Greenhaven Press
27500 Drake Rd.
Farmington Hills, MI 48331-3535
Or you can visit our Internet site at http://www.gale.com

LIBRARY OF CONGRESS CATALOGING-IN-PUBLICATION DATA

Obesity / Tom and Gena Metcalf, book editors.
   p. cm. — (Perspectives on diseases and disorders)
Includes bibliographical references and index.
ISBN 978-0-7377-3873-5 (hardcover)
1. Obesity—Popular works. I. Metcalf, Tom.
RC628.O218 2008
616.3'98—dc22

2007037470

ISBN-10: 0-7377-3873-1

Printed in the United States of America

CONTENTS

INTRODUCTION

According to a study published in 2006, "an estimated 64.5 percent of Americans older than 20 years are overweight." With an ever-expanding population, obesity can be a sensitive subject. Parents of an obese child may elicit looks of judgment by fellow shoppers in a supermarket; an overweight teenager may feel ostracized by his peers. With the overwhelming amount of information flooding the media and other outlets, obesity is one disease that everyone feels they are an expert on. The question of whether obesity is an issue to be dealt with within society has long since been decided in the affirmative, but the exact role of society is still yet to be determined.

One issue that comes to the forefront in this debate is the rising cost of health care. Some critics claim that the influx of obesity-related illness has the potential to put an increased strain on the health care system—whether through rising health care costs or other costs. For example, the legislature in Australia put forth in 2006 a $25 million "anti-obesity" initiative, with about $3 million of that going toward larger ambulances, heavy-duty stretchers, and other medical equipment designed for obese patients. Proponents of the measure would be quick to point out that $10 million of the initiative would go to preventative measures, such as healthy eating and wellness programs. While some may see the value in the preventative measures, many would ask if catering to the obese is helpful or simply enabling ever-expanding waistlines.

Dr. Raul Uppot studied the effects of obesity on one specific aspect of health care, X-rays, by examining image quality and reviewing radiology reports taken between

1998 and 2003. The report points to poorer quality of images in obese patients, increasing the chance that these patients may be misdiagnosed or that they may have increased office visits to determine a course of action. In addition, the report underscores the strain that obese patients put on hospital workers and equipment. According to the study "approximately 83% of technologists have reported some pain when moving obese patients." Also, some obese patients are unable to fit on computed tomography (CT) or magnetic resonance (MRI) imaging tables—which impacts patient care as well as hospital budgets and administrators who are faced with purchasing new equipment.

Though the radiological study produced clear results, the resulting action necessary by doctors, hospitals, and

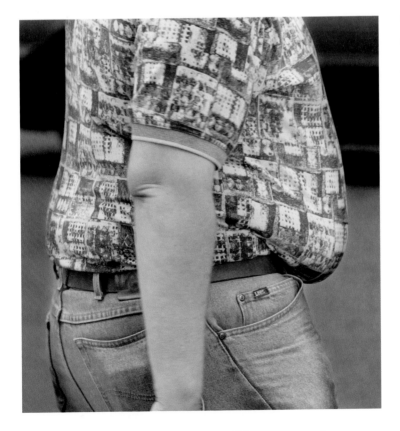

The obesity epidemic affects millions of people every day.
(AP Images)

patients is less clear. Treating obese patients is increasingly a matter of balancing the needs and well-being of patients, hospital workers, and administrators. According to Uppot:

> The short term solution is the responsibility of radiologists, hospitals, and equipment manufacturers to accommodate obese patients and obtain high quality images by learning how to adjust the current equipment settings and redesigning equipment to accommodate larger patients.
>
> The long term solution is the responsibility of patients to have a good diet and exercise and to lose weight so that their care is not hindered in the hospital.

As Uppot suggests, the solution to the growing concern among health care officials is likely two-pronged—decreasing the prevalence of obesity, which requires some initiative on the part of patients, as well as new accommodations made by the health care industry.

The role of other societal accommodations made for the obese is more ambiguous. Seating on airplanes, in theaters, and other social settings has become a real issue for the obese. In the case of airplane seating and aisleways, it is no secret that airlines are reducing the size of both in an effort to increase the number of seats on planes. The reduction of legroom and narrower seats can make even an average-size passenger uncomfortable. According to a 2002 BBC report, the "average economy seats on the ten most popular airlines is less than 18 inches"—though some planes were found to have seats as narrow as 15 inches.

Advocates for the obese have called for wider seats to accommodate every passenger. The concern may go beyond comfort. In emergency situations, passengers who are squished into too small seats may have a more difficult time exiting their seats; narrow aisleways may pose a risk for larger passengers to navigate. In addition, larger passengers who are forced to squeeze into narrow seats may be at a higher risk for deep vein thrombosis (DVT). According to a 2002 Civil Aviation Authority (CAA) survey, "[A narrow seat] restricts the opportunity for passengers to change posture, not only because of the limited space but also because of the disturbance it may cause the adjacent passenger." The survey recommends that seat width be increased to a minimum of 20 inches, with 23 inches being the ideal.

The trade-off for making such adjustments may mean more comfort for all, but it may also result in increased ticket prices. Increasing seat width will undoubtedly mean fewer seats per plane, which means that passengers could expect to pay more per trip. Since the cost would be passed on to all passengers, the change remains controversial, with many arguing that an obese passenger should simply pay more for a first-class ticket, which typically has roomier seats. But the issues brought up by the CAA about passenger safety raises concerns that this issue is one that all passengers should care about. In the event of an emergency, for example, it is imperative that all passengers exit the plane in a quick and orderly manner. One passenger could impact the safety of many others.

Whether it is the rising cost of health care or an issue that seems further removed, such as the potential for soaring airline ticket prices, obesity is a concern that affects all citizens. The issue cannot be ignored, and passing judgment or pointing fingers will only exacerbate an already difficult subject. Although the first reaction may be to place responsibility with the obese person, the obesity epidemic is only growing year after year and must be addressed in a way that is sensitive and logical for all.

CHAPTER 1

Understanding Obesity

Obesity: An Overview

Rosalyn Carson-DeWitt and Rebecca J. Frey

Dr. Rosalyn Carson-DeWitt and Dr. Rebecca Frey define obesity by the body mass index (BMI), citing statistics to show the epidemic proportions of the problem. They discuss the processes by which the body converts food to fat. The authors list fourteen different diseases and conditions that are a direct result of obesity and note that treatment for obesity focuses on behavior modification and doctor-supervised dieting. Alternative medicines such as Chinese herbs are discussed as well. The authors note that the key to prevention, according to obesity experts, may be controlling rather than counting calories.

Obesity is an abnormal accumulation of body fat, usually 20% or more over an individual's ideal body weight. Obesity is associated with increased risk of illness, disability, and death. The branch of medicine that deals with the study and treatment of obesity is

Photo on facing page. Teens and children falling into the highest weight category may be considered "obese" if the American Medical Association changes the classification from the current label, "overweight." **(AP images)**

SOURCE: Rosalyn Carson-DeWitt and Rebecca J. Frey, "Obesity," *Gale Encyclopedia of Medicine*, Farmington Hills, MI: Thomson Gale, 2006. Reproduced by permission of Thomson Gale.

known as bariatrics. As obesity has become a major health problem in the United States, bariatrics has become a separate medical and surgical specialty.

Obesity traditionally has been defined as a weight at least 20% above the weight corresponding to the lowest death rate for individuals of a specific height, gender, and age (ideal weight). Twenty to forty percent over ideal weight is considered mildly obese; 40–100% over ideal weight is considered moderately obese; and 100% over ideal weight is considered severely, or morbidly, obese. More recent guidelines for obesity use a measurement called BMI (body mass index) which is the individual's weight multiplied by 703 and then divided by twice the height in inches. BMI of 25.9–29 is considered overweight; BMI over 30 is considered obese. Measurements and comparisons of waist and hip circumference can also provide some information regarding risk factors associated with weight. The higher the ratio, the greater the chance for weight-associated complications. Calipers can be used to measure skin-fold thickness to determine whether tissue is muscle (lean) or adipose tissue (fat).

Much concern has been generated about the increasing incidence of obesity among Americans. Some studies have noted an increase from 12% to 18% occurring between 1991 and 1998. Other studies have actually estimated that a full 50% of all Americans are overweight. The World Health Organization terms obesity a worldwide epidemic, and the diseases which can occur due to obesity are becoming increasingly prevalent.

Excessive weight can result in many serious, potentially life-threatening health problems, including hypertension, Type II diabetes mellitus (non-insulin dependent diabetes), increased risk for coronary disease, increased unexplained

FAST FACT

In 2005, 1.6 billion adults were overweight worldwide. The World Health Organization estimates 2.3 billion adults will be overweight by 2015.

heart attack, hyperlipidemia, infertility, and a higher prevalence of colon, prostate, endometrial, and, possibly, breast cancer. Approximately 300,000 deaths a year are attributed to obesity, prompting leaders in public health, such as former Surgeon General C. Everett Koop, M.D., to label obesity "the second leading cause of preventable deaths in the United States."

Obesity Is the Result of Many Factors

The mechanism for excessive weight gain is clear—more calories are consumed than the body burns, and the excess calories are stored as fat (adipose) tissue. However, the exact cause is not as clear and likely arises from a complex combination of factors. Genetic factors significantly influence how the body regulates the appetite and the rate at which it turns food into energy (metabolic rate). Studies of adoptees confirm this relationship— the majority of adoptees followed a pattern of weight gain that more closely resembled that of their birth parents than their adoptive parents. A genetic predisposition to weight gain, however, does not automatically mean that a person will be obese. Eating habits and patterns of physical activity also play a significant role in the amount of weight a person gains. Recent studies have indicated that the amount of fat in a person's diet may have a greater impact on weight than the number of calories it contains.

Carbohydrates like cereals, breads, fruits, and vegetables and protein (fish, lean meat, turkey breast, skim milk) are converted to fuel almost as soon as they are consumed. Most fat calories are immediately stored in fat cells, which add to the body's weight and girth as they expand and multiply. A sedentary lifestyle, particularly prevalent in affluent societies, such as in the United States, can contribute to weight gain. Psychological factors, such as depression and low self-esteem may, in some cases, also play a role in weight gain.

Body Mass Index (BMI) Table

BMI	19	20	21	22	23	24	25	26	27	28	29	30	31	32	33	34	35
Height							*Weight (in pounds)*										
4'10" (58")	91	96	100	105	110	115	119	124	129	134	138	143	148	153	158	162	167
4'11" (59")	94	99	104	109	114	119	124	128	133	138	143	148	153	158	163	168	173
5' (60")	97	102	107	112	118	123	128	133	138	143	148	153	158	163	168	174	179
5'1" (61")	100	106	111	116	122	127	132	137	143	148	153	158	164	169	174	180	185
5'2" (62")	104	109	115	120	126	131	136	142	147	153	158	164	169	175	180	186	191
5'3" (63")	107	113	118	124	130	135	141	146	152	158	163	169	175	180	186	191	197
5'4" (64")	110	116	122	128	134	140	145	151	157	163	169	174	180	186	192	197	204
5'5" (65")	114	120	126	132	138	144	150	156	162	168	174	180	186	192	198	204	210
5'6" (66")	118	124	130	136	142	148	155	161	167	173	179	186	192	198	204	210	216
5'7" (67")	121	127	134	140	146	153	159	166	172	178	185	191	198	204	211	217	223
5'8" (68")	125	131	138	144	151	158	164	171	177	184	190	197	203	210	216	223	230
5'9" (69")	128	135	142	149	155	162	169	176	182	189	196	203	209	216	223	230	236
5'10" (70")	132	139	146	153	160	167	174	181	188	195	202	209	216	222	229	236	243
5'11" (71")	136	143	150	157	165	172	179	186	193	200	208	215	222	229	236	243	250
6' (72")	140	147	154	162	169	177	184	191	199	206	213	221	228	235	242	250	258
6'1" (73")	144	151	159	166	174	182	189	197	204	212	219	227	235	242	250	257	265
6'2" (74")	148	155	163	171	179	186	194	202	210	218	225	233	241	249	256	264	272
6'3" (75")	152	160	168	176	184	192	200	208	216	224	232	240	248	256	264	272	279

Source: Evidence Report of Clinical Guidelines on the Identification, Evaluation, and Treatment of Overweight and Obesity in Adults, 1998. NIH/National Heart, Lung, and Blood Institute (NHLBI).

At what stage of life a person becomes obese can affect his or her ability to lose weight. In childhood, excess calories are converted into new fat cells (hyperplastic obesity), while excess calories consumed in adulthood only serve to expand existing fat cells (hypertrophic obesity).

Since dieting and exercise can only reduce the size of fat cells, not eliminate them, persons who were obese as children can have great difficulty losing weight, since they may have up to five times as many fat cells as someone who became overweight as an adult.

Obesity Is Associated with Many Disorders

Obesity can also be a side effect of certain disorders and conditions, including:

- Cushing's syndrome, a disorder involving the excessive release of the hormone cortisol
- hypothyroidism, a condition caused by an underactive thyroid gland
- neurologic disturbances, such as damage to the hypothalamus, a structure located deep within the brain that helps regulate appetite
- consumption of such drugs as steroids, antipsychotic medications, or antidepressants

The major symptoms of obesity are excessive weight gain and the presence of large amounts of fatty tissue. Obesity can also give rise to several secondary conditions, including:

- arthritis and other orthopedic problems, such as lower back pain
- hernias
- heartburn
- adult-onset asthma
- gum disease

- high cholesterol levels
- gallstones
- high blood pressure
- menstrual irregularities or cessation of menstruation (amenorrhea)
- decreased fertility, and pregnancy complications
- shortness of breath that can be incapacitating
- sleep apnea and sleeping disorders
- skin disorders arising from the bacterial breakdown of sweat and cellular material in thick folds of skin or from increased friction between folds
- emotional and social problems

Successful Treatment Takes a Lifetime

Treatment of obesity depends primarily on how overweight a person is and his or her overall health. However, to be successful, any treatment must affect life-long behavioral changes rather than short-term weight loss. "Yo-yo" dieting, in which weight is repeatedly lost and regained, has been shown to increase a person's likelihood of developing fatal health problems than if the weight had been lost gradually or not lost at all. Behavior-focused treatment should concentrate on:

- What and how much a person eats. This aspect may involve keeping a food diary and developing a better understanding of the nutritional value and fat content of foods. It may also involve changing grocery-shopping habits (e.g., buying only what is on a prepared list and only going on a certain day), timing of meals (to prevent feelings of hunger, a person may plan frequent, small meals), and actually slowing down the rate at which a person eats.
- How a person responds to food. This may involve understanding what psychological issues underlie a

person's eating habits. For example, one person may binge eat when under stress, while another may always use food as a reward. In recognizing these psychological triggers, an individual can develop alternate coping mechanisms that do not focus on food.

- How they spend their time. Making activity and exercise an integrated part of everyday life is a key to achieving and maintaining weight loss. Starting slowly and building endurance keeps individuals from becoming discouraged. Varying routines and trying new activities also keeps interest high.

For most individuals who are mildly obese, these behavior modifications entail life-style changes they can make independently while being supervised by a family physician. Other mildly obese persons may seek the help of a commercial weight-loss program (e.g., Weight Watchers). The effectiveness of these programs is difficult to assess, since programs vary widely, drop-out rates are high, and few employ members of the medical community. However, programs that emphasize realistic goals, gradual progress, sensible eating, and exercise can be very helpful and are recommended by many doctors. Programs that promise instant weight loss or feature severely restricted diets are not effective and, in some cases, can be dangerous.

For individuals who are moderately obese, medically supervised behavior modification and weight loss are required. While doctors will put most moderately obese patients on a balanced, low-calorie diet (1200–1500 calories a day), they may recommend that certain individuals follow a very-low-calorie liquid protein diet (400–700 calories) for as long as three months. This therapy, however, should not be confused with commercial liquid protein diets or commercial weight-loss shakes and drinks. Doctors tailor these diets to specific patients, monitor patients carefully, and use them for only a short period of time. In addition to reducing the amount and type of calories consumed by the patient, doctors will recommend professional therapists or psychiatrists who can help the individual effectively change his or her behavior in regard to eating.

For individuals who are severely obese, dietary changes and behavior modification may be accompanied by surgery to reduce or bypass portions of the stomach or small intestine. Although obesity surgery is less risky as of 2003 because of recent innovations in equipment and surgical technique, it is still performed only on patients for whom other strategies have failed and whose obesity seriously threatens their health. Other surgical

Surgery has become a popular option among people who are overweight. (AP Images)

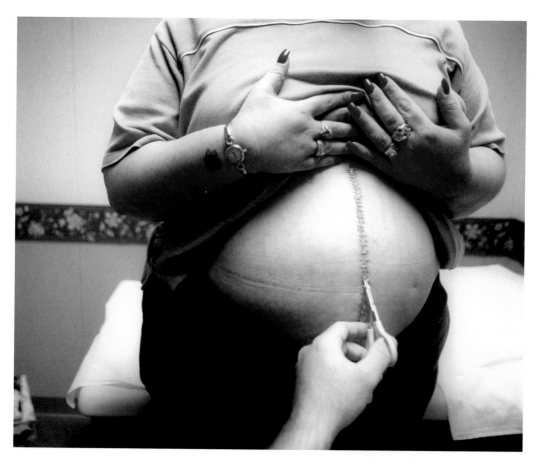

procedures are not recommended, including liposuction, a purely cosmetic procedure in which a suction device is used to remove fat from beneath the skin, and jaw wiring, which can damage gums and teeth and cause painful muscle spasms.

Appetite-suppressant drugs are sometimes prescribed to aid in weight loss. These drugs work by increasing levels of serotonin or catecholamine, which are brain chemicals that control feelings of fullness. Appetite suppressants, though, are not considered truly effective, since most of the weight lost while taking them is usually regained after stopping them. Also, suppressants containing amphetamines can be potentially abused by patients. While most of the immediate side-effects of these drugs are harmless, the long-term effects of these drugs, in many cases, are unknown.

Obesity Causes and Treatments

Lester Crawford

Lester Crawford is a doctor of veterinary medicine and a PhD scientist. He was the acting director of the Food and Drug Administration (FDA) when he addressed the World Obesity Congress and Expo in 2004. This selection is excerpted from his keynote address. In it Crawford expresses concern about the increasing number of overweight people both in the United States and around the world. He reviews the work done by an FDA study group, which concluded that the causes of obesity are varied. The group reached the conclusion that obesity would not be solved easily.

At the FDA, we are accountable for the safety and the wholesome nature of 80 percent of our national food supply—practically everything we eat except for beef, poultry, and a few egg products. This responsibility, in addition to our general duty to protect and promote the public health, has placed our agency in

SOURCE: Lester Crawford, DVM, PhD, "Keynote Address," World Obesity Congress & Expo, 2004.

the forefront of our government's efforts to bring the runaway excess-weight problem under control.

And a major problem it is: overweight and obesity affect about two out of every three Americans—and, what is even more alarming, 15 percent of our children and adolescents. These extra pounds are ruinous to health by increasing the risks for a host of diseases that are inflating our nation's morbidity and mortality statistics. According to the most recent estimates, obesity is a causative factor in as many as 400,000 deaths each year, which makes it the second most devastating avoidable cause of premature death in [the] United States after tobacco.

Moreover, while smoking is on the decline, overweight and obesity statistics are relentlessly rising, and threaten to erode the substantial gains in life expectancy and quality of life that have been won by modern medicine. While the resulting human suffering is the most dire aspect of this epidemic, its economic consequences accentuate the hardship. The costs of obesity-associated health care and lost productivity are currently estimated at $117 billion a year.

A Tremendous Challenge

For us at the FDA, this ominous drift into disease and expense presents a tremendous challenge that—although not at our doorsteps alone—we know we must confront with all available powers and resources. Last August [2003], we therefore appointed an expert Obesity Working Group and charged it with two basic tasks: exploring the critical dimensions of the excess-weight problem, and devising a plan on how to address it.

The group's probe was a major undertaking. Our working group consisted of 17 FDA senior scientists and staffers who were backed by more than 40 specialists researching the various issues under study. We were briefed by experts from other government agencies; consulted with the public and academia; met with representatives

Possible Contributors to Weight Gain

Sleep debt can lead to weight gain

Pollution affects our hormones, which control our weight

Air conditioning does the work of controlling body temperature for us

Decreased instances of smoking; smoking reduces weight

Older mothers lend more chance of obesity to their children than young mothers

Obese parents are likely to pass on the condition to their offspring

Source: S.W. Keith, *International Journal of Obesity*, advance online publication, June 27, 2006. www.webmd.com/diet/news/20060627/obesity-more-complex-than-we-think.

of the packaged food and restaurant industries; and solicited and reviewed scores of expert comments on various aspects of the obesity epidemic....

What have we learned? The overriding lesson of our inquiry is that the epidemic has no single cause: rather, it is the confluence of numerous factors acting together over time. Ergo, our second key conclusion is that the epidemic will have no simple or speedy solution. Controlling obesity will be [a] long-term process requiring coordinated and comprehensive efforts on many fronts.

One of the most surprising findings was that a large part of our population is not even aware that excessive weight is a health problem. Evidence reviewed by our group indicates that both adults and teenagers frequently misperceive their weight status, and that this misperception cuts across gender, socioeconomic status, age and ethnicity.

PERSPECTIVES ON DISEASES AND DISORDERS

This is particularly true about individuals who regard themselves as overweight rather than obese. Recent focus group studies indicate that these men and women generally brush off the extra pounds as of minor significance, and therefore have little incentive to get rid of them. Raising the public's consciousness that excessive avoirs-du-pois are a serious health hazard is our foremost, urgent task.

The Connection Between Diet and Health

Another big hurdle to be overcome is the inaccurate assessment by many consumers of their diets' implications for their health. For example, a survey of the U.S. Department of Agriculture has found that four out of ten people who cook at home have an exaggerated opinion of the nutritional quality of the meals they prepare. Other research has shown that many parents significantly underestimate how often their children snack between regular mealtimes. A large segment of our public appears to lack—or even care about—accurate information about their nutrition.

This was reflected in the disappointing effectiveness of the current food label, which shows how the major nutrients in each food package fit into a healthy daily diet of 2,000 or 2,500 calories. When it was first introduced, more than 10 years ago, fewer than 56 percent of Americans were overweight, and fewer than 23 percent were obese. It was then estimated that the implied dietary advice on the label would prevent many of the then-300,000 overweight-related deaths a year, and save up to $13 billion in health care costs in a decade.

Today, we know better. . . .

Over time, and particularly in recent years, the medical community has come to recognize that short-term measures to address obesity don't adequately reduce the long-term risks associated with excess weight. As we all

FAST FACT

Obesity is associated with at least fifteen medical conditions. Some of these are osteoarthritis, cancer, cardiovascular disease, hypertension, joint-related pain, strokes, and impaired immune response (less resistance to harmful organisms).

now know and understand, obesity is a chronic condition associated with wide-ranging derangements of energy metabolism. Over the long term, that increases the risk for numerous serious and life-threatening diseases.

Based on this understanding, and following the recommendations of an advisory committee, our agency in 1996 issued a draft guidance that set the framework for the development of chronic-use drugs to treat obesity. The document called for long-term clinical trials of safety and efficacy, and set forth standards of effectiveness in the hope of fostering the development of a crop of chronic-use preventives and remedies that would ultimately reduce the disease risks of obesity.

Since then, our agency has approved three long-term treatments for weight control: dexfenfluramine, sibutramine and orlistat. Dexfenfluramine, which took the market by storm in a popular combination regimen with phentermine, was withdrawn within 18 months of approval after it was shown to be associated with valvulopathy. This was an effect not predicted by any of the premarket data, whether in animals or in patients. Sibutramine is an effective drug, but it causes increases in pulse and blood pressure in some individuals, and requires careful monitoring. Orlistat, like sibutramine, is modestly effective, though apparently very safe.

The Need for Drug-Based Treatments

In sum, a highly effective drug-based treatment for overweight and obesity is, today, sorely lacking in the medical armamentarium [tools for treatment]. Available therapies are only modestly effective, by no means so in all treated patients, and have no lasting effect once the use of the drug is stopped, thus necessitating lifelong therapy in many individuals. We have no cure for obesity. Furthermore, there has never been a therapeutic class whose progress has been more vehemently buffeted by opposing desires for a true cure and concerns about drug risk—concerns that are frequently accompanied by arguments that obesity should be addressed with behavior modification. Obesity therapeutics is an exceedingly difficult area in which to work.

At the same time, one of the most encouraging conclusions of our Working Group is that opportunities for safer and more effective obesity drugs abound, and that

States like West Virginia have taken up the challenge to erase obesity by posting billboards and creating programs available to all. (AP Images)

the future of weight-control therapies is potentially bright. The list of molecular targets and mechanistic approaches is long, and grows daily thanks to vigorous basic research in this field. We have good reasons to hope for the development of safe and effective single-drug therapies and combination regimens to assist people in achieving and maintaining healthy weight. . . .

The Health Care Industry Must Act

I'll mention some of the basic topics that require exploration and debate:

- First and foremost, we have no evidence from clinical trials that weight loss induced by any of the available obesity drugs reduces risk for long-term serious morbid—such as cardiovascular disease—and mortal consequences of the condition. It is of essence that plans to address this critical question be developed as soon as possible.

- Reliance on weight loss alone as the measure of efficacy would seem to require large, long-term exposures for providing at least presumptive evidence of benefits outweighing risks. This is particularly true because historically, the benefits of these drugs have been on the average small, and by no means universal. This is clearly a barrier that must be discussed.

- Given our limited armamentarium for obesity and the critical health effects and prevalence of the condition, we believe that head-to-head comparisons of new and existing treatments are critical for progress. It is, for example, disconcerting that the most frequently prescribed obesity drug in the U.S. today is phentermine. It is a drug that's approved for short-term use, but clearly is prescribed chronically, and we have neither information on its long-term safety nor on its efficacy when compared to more recently approved chronic-use products.

• In addition, we need to discuss the conduct of studies of combination therapies, and of trials to examine the safety and effectiveness of drug cycling. We need to address these issues for both new and previously approved therapies.

After six months of intensive consultations and research, our Obesity Working Group concluded that the stark reality of the obesity epidemic, and its deleterious consequences for health, constitute a call to action for the entire health care community—pharmaceutical industry, academia, health care professionals, as well as FDA and its sister public health agencies.

The Modern Lifestyle
Contributes to Obesity

Sarah Aase

In the following article Sarah Aase highlights the growing problem of teenage obesity. She cites a statistic that one-third of all teenagers are at risk of developing heart disease because they are overweight and out of shape. According to Aase, sedentary lifestyles are partly to blame, as people walk and exercise less and spend more time in front of the television or computer. Fattening food choices are also partly to blame. Food companies, she says, spend about half of their advertising dollars marketing to children. Fast-food restaurants are more likely to be located near schools. As people learn more about the dangers of obesity, school officials and others are acting to promote good nutrition and exercise.

Shawna R. was 14 years old and weighed 270 pounds when she found out she needed to lower her blood sugar. "The doctor told me if I didn't

SOURCE: Sarah Aase, "The Problem with Obesity: Are Our Lifestyles Setting Us Up for Shorter Lives?" *Current Health 2*, vol. 33, November 2006, pp. 8–12. Copyright © 2006 Weekly Reader Corp. Reproduced by permission.

start to get healthier, I would become diabetic in the next couple of years," says the Haydenville, Mass., sophomore. Shawna's extra weight had bothered her since fifth grade, but her doctor's words pushed her to action. "That really scared me."

Shawna isn't alone. "Over the last 20 years, we have seen a radical increase in obesity," says S. Bryn Austin of Children's Hospital in Boston. In fact, three times as many teens are overweight today as were about 25 years ago.

Too Much Fat Disrupts Normal Body Functions

Fat cells store and release energy into the bloodstream, along with hormones and other compounds that help regulate your body's systems. When you take in more calories than you burn, fat cells start to swell and multiply. More fat requires more blood, which strains your circulatory system. Excess weight around your joints and windpipe make it harder for you to walk and breathe.

Ballooning fat cells also cause your body's normal chemical signals to go haywire. Too many fat cells make the brain less responsive to signals that the stomach is full. They also interfere with the way the body processes food and release chemicals that can damage the heart, liver, and muscle cells. Doctors are seeing more teens with serious health problems. Some include high blood pressure, fatty liver disease (a buildup of fat in the liver), type 2 diabetes, and signs of artery hardening—all conditions that can lead to heart disease and stroke.

That spells trouble for many overweight and obese teens. Last year [2005], a nationwide study found that at least one-third, or 7.5 million teens, are so out of shape that they are at significant risk of developing heart disease.

> ## FAST FACT
>
> According to the National Business Group on Health, obesity costs employers $13 billion a year and results in 39 million lost workdays.

And the Centers for Disease Control and Prevention released a 30-minute video called *The Biggest Generation*, which warned that today's children may have shorter life spans than their parents.

Inactive Lifestyles Add to Obesity

Some experts lay part of the blame for obesity on technological advances. "People used to have to work pretty hard to get their food. Now we have to make an effort to be physically active," says Dianne Neumark-Sztainer, an epidemiologist at the University of Minnesota. At the same time entrepreneurs were creating more types of fast food, people also started moving less, driving more, and watching more TV. One in every two kids walked or biked to school 30 years ago, but today, just one in eight does.

Being sedentary (not getting enough physical activity) isn't the only reason people gain weight, though.

Active children are less likely to develop obesity. (AP Images)

Food is a major culprit. Just in the past 20 years, the range of convenience-food choices has exploded. Yes, McDonald's and Dairy Queen existed in the 1980s, but not Starbucks, Chipotle, or Jamba Juice, let alone food courts or vending machines in schools.

Food Companies and Restaurants Target Children

And food companies want your money. Roughly half of all U.S. advertising directed at children and teens is for food, with estimated sales exceeding $27 billion in 2002. In a study of Chicago-area schools, Austin and her colleagues found that fast-food restaurants were "three to four times more concentrated around schools" than those that were randomly located, she says. Given these factors and today's busy lifestyles, it's no wonder that teens are eating out more than they used to.

That's not a good thing. Not only are convenience foods higher in calories and saturated fat than home-cooked meals, but their portion sizes also have ballooned. For example, 20 years ago, a cheeseburger had 333 calories. Today, it has 590. Overall, boys and girls are eating an average of 243 and 123 more calories per day, respectively, than their parents did. Consider that 3,500 calories make up a pound of fat, and you can see how easy it is to gain weight.

Losing Weight Is a Life-Changing Event

Nobody knows that better than Jahcobie C. Last fall [2005], at 5 feet 10 inches and 483 pounds, the Boston native may have been one of the heaviest 15-year-olds in the world. "I would eat 10 McChickens, five apple pies, three large fries, and a Diet Coke," Jahcobie says. "The most food I could get for the cheapest amount of money is what I would eat."

For Shawna and Jahcobie, the turning point came when they each won a scholarship through Louie's Kids,

Obesity-Related Diseases

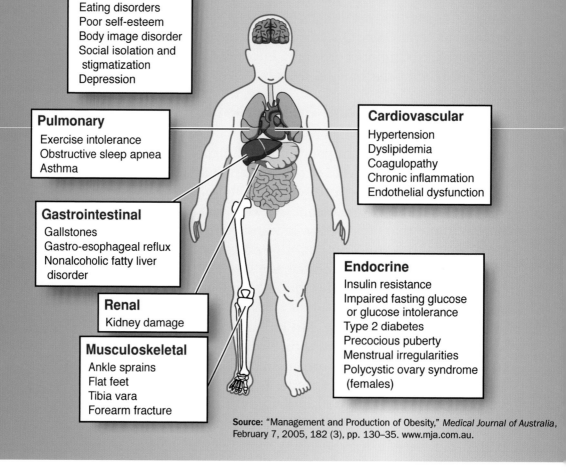

Psychosocial

Eating disorders
Poor self-esteem
Body image disorder
Social isolation and
  stigmatization
Depression

Pulmonary

Exercise intolerance
Obstructive sleep apnea
Asthma

Gastrointestinal

Gallstones
Gastro-esophageal reflux
Nonalcoholic fatty liver
  disorder

Renal

Kidney damage

Musculoskeletal

Ankle sprains
Flat feet
Tibia vara
Forearm fracture

Cardiovascular

Hypertension
Dyslipidemia
Coagulopathy
Chronic inflammation
Endothelial dysfunction

Endocrine

Insulin resistance
Impaired fasting glucose
  or glucose intolerance
Type 2 diabetes
Precocious puberty
Menstrual irregularities
Polycystic ovary syndrome
  (females)

Source: "Management and Production of Obesity," *Medical Journal of Australia*, February 7, 2005, 182 (3), pp. 130–35. www.mja.com.au.

a nonprofit organization that sends teens to weight-loss camps and schools. Shawna attended the month-long Wellspring summer camp in Canton, N.C. Now 15, she has shed 90 pounds and reduced her risk of developing type 2 diabetes. Jahcobie spent eight months at the Reedley, Calif.–based boarding school Academy of the Sierras, where he learned a lot about healthy weight-loss strategies. Currently 16, Jahcobie has lost 170 pounds and plans to lose 115 more over the next 18 months.

Both teens say the experiences taught them how to eat well, how to make exercise a part of their daily lives, and how to let go of food as a comfort device. As Jahcobie and Shawna lost weight, each gained a healthy new relationship with food.

The Body Mass Index Measures Healthy Weight

Researchers use a measurement called body mass index (BMI), a ratio of weight to height. A person's BMI is compared against those of other people the same sex and age. Then it is ranked to determine what a healthy weight is.

"BMI is not a perfect indicator and should be followed up with a doctor or nurse," says Virginia Chomitz, senior scientist at the Institute for Community Health of Cambridge, Mass. For instance, a 15-year-old boy who is 5 feet 10 inches tall and weighs 150 pounds would fall into the at-risk category if he gained 20 pounds. But if the weight is muscle mass, that's a good thing. See the BMI calculator that's designed just for kids and teens at the Centers for Disease Control and Prevention's Web site at apps.nccd.cdc.gov/dnpabmi/Calculator.aspx.

FAST FACT

Over one hundred NFL quarterbacks have a BMI of at least 25. The standard for overweight is a BMI of 25 and over.

Across the Country People Are Fighting Obesity

Across the country, school and health officials are trying different approaches to curb teen obesity. Arkansas officials weigh students and send home information about their body-mass index; California officials are raising the nutritional standards of school meals; West Virginia officials are purchasing dance video games for all public schools; and a group of soft-drink manufacturers has agreed to stop selling all but low-calorie soft drinks in schools within a few years.

Body Chemistry Contributes to Obesity

Weill Medical College Newsletter

The following article is from a newsletter published by the Weill Medical College of Cornell University. In it Dr. Louis Aronne, a professor at the college and the director of the weight-control program at New York Presbyterian Hospital–Weill Cornell Medical Center, discusses the role of body chemistry in weight control. The body's endocannabinoid system malfunctions and makes one feel hungry, even when full, Aronne explains. Endocannabinoids may also help to bring on the condition of pre-diabetes. While drugs are under consideration by the FDA (Food and Drug Administration) to treat the condition, Aronne recommends changing behavior as a better way to trick an overactive endocannabinoid system. These behavioral changes include eating smaller portions of food and eating foods with high fiber content. Exercise, he says, is important to balance the body's tendency to burn fewer calories when food intake is reduced.

SOURCE: Weill Medical College Newsletter, "Body Weight and Body Chemistry," vol. 10, February 2007, pp. 1, 8. Reproduced by permission.

Ever had the munchies even after you just ate? That urge to snack may be due to an overactive chemical "feedback" system that regulates appetite, food intake, fat metabolism, and body weight. The chemical culprit is called the endocannabinoid (EC) system, and it's the latest target in medicine's battle of the bulge. We can't change the EC system, but we may be able to work around it by defusing cues to overeat.

Obesity Is Biochemically Based

"What many people have traditionally viewed as a lack of willpower could actually have a biochemical basis," says Louis J. Aronne, MD, director of the Comprehensive Weight Control Program at New York Presbyterian Hospital-Weill Cornell Medical Center and a clinical professor of medicine at Weill Medical College of Cornell University in New York. "It's not just a matter of lack of willpower to stop eating, or of an obesity drug not working, but the body's counterbalancing mechanisms that stops people from losing weight."

When your EC system is activated, it increases hunger and decreases satiety [a feeling of fullness], driving the desire for tasty food, says Dr. Aronne. He calls this the "feed-forward" mechanism. "When you eat a high-fat, high-carbohydrate food, it activates the endocannabinoid system, leading you to eat even more," he explains. "The endocannabinoid system interacts with other hormones to make you feel hungrier, increases body fat, and drives weight gain. We now know that the endocannabinoid system is overactive in obese people. In one study, obese women were found to have higher levels of endocannabinoids than lean women."

"Munchie" Receptors

Endocannabinoids are akin to the active chemical (*cannabinoids*) in marijuana that triggers its effects, including the "munchies." There are cannabinoid receptors all over the body—including the brain, the gastrointestinal tract, and fat cells. When cannabinoid receptors are activated in the brain (in the *hypothalamus*), it stimulates appetite, leading to increased food intake, says Dr. Aronne.

In the gastrointestinal system, activated cannabinoid receptors interact with insulin, the hormone that brings energy from food into cells as glucose, to inhibit its effects. An overactive EC system impairs the ability of cells, especially muscle cells, to use insulin, leading to insulin resistance, the precursor to type 2 diabetes. Activating cannabinoid receptors in fat cells triggers triglyceride production, increased fat accumulation, and weight gain.

What You Can Do

To combat the "feed forward" urge and stop mindless overeating:

✓ **Consume foods that are low in calories but high in fiber** and water to help make you feel fuller.

✓ **Use smaller plates and serving utensils** to control portion sizes.

✓ **Beware of the "clean plate" mentality**; visualize how much you're going to eat before you start eating.

✓ **Avoid all-you-can-eat restaurants and buffets**; they promote overeating.

✓ **Eat slowly**; it takes the brain 20 minutes to sense that you're full.

✓ **Don't do other activities while you eat**, such as watching TV.

Source: *Food & Fitness Advisor*, Weill Medical College of Cornell University, February 2007.

"It also appears that overactivating the EC system leads to laying down of fat in the liver, which is a key factor in insulin resistance," says Dr. Aronne. "There is also data to show that insulin and the hormone *leptin*, which are important signals to the brain telling how much nutrition has come in and how much fat is stored, also interact with the EC system."

Blocking Receptors

Blocking cannabinoid receptors may dampen an overactive EC system, reining in appetite, reducing weight, and improving obesity-related risk factors for heart disease and type 2 diabetes.

A drug that blocks cannabinoid receptors, *rimonabant (Acomplia)*, is being considered by the U.S. Food and Drug Administration (FDA) to treat people with type 2 diabetes. Four similar drugs are also in the pipeline. "We've seen that blocking these receptors results not only in reduction of food intake, but also a reduction in triglycerides and glucose, and even an increase in 'good' HDL cholesterol. And that's above and beyond any reduction in weight," says Dr. Aronne.

A recent review of four placebo-controlled clinical trials of rimonabant found it produces only moderate weight loss. But even the average 5 percent weight loss seen in the trials after one year of using 5 mg of rimonabant reduced risk factors for type 2 diabetes and cardiovascular disease, according to the October 17, 2006 edition of *The Cochrane Library*.

A higher dose (20 mg) produced a larger weight loss, almost 11 pounds, as well as a reduction in waist circumference, triglycerides, blood pressure, and raised low HDL cholesterol. These are all risk factors for metabolic syndrome, notes Dr. Aronne.

"In the clinical trial conducted in North America, there was a 39 percent reduction in metabolic syndrome prevalence in the rimonabant group versus 8 percent in the placebo group." However, the higher dose also produced more side effects such as dizziness, nausea, headache, and depressed mood.

What Can You Do?

Aside from taking medication such as rimonabant to block EC receptors, *sibutramine (Meridia)* to enhance satiety and reduce appetite, or block fat absorption with *orlistat* (*Xenical,* soon to be over the counter), you can't really alter your body chemistry, says Dr. Aronne. Both Meridia and Xenical result in an average 6–10 pounds more weight loss than placebo.

However, you can use knowledge about the EC system to help you work around it. For example, nutritionists have a number of proven strategies that can help you defuse the urge to snack or overeat, such as waiting 5–15 minutes for a craving to pass, distracting yourself with other activities (such as taking a walk), or even drinking a glass of water. If you're able to satisfy a craving with just a small portion of a treat, then have it.

Choose foods that help increase your sense of fullness, those high in water and rich in fiber, such as fruits and vegetables; eating a piece of fruit can also help satisfy a craving for sweets. Realize that it takes the brain 20 minutes to sense that you're full. Slow down when you eat; it promotes satiety and increases enjoyment.

A 2003 study suggests that exercise may activate cannabinoid receptors, partly accounting for the "runners' high" and for increased appetite after a workout. So if you're usually ravenous after exercising, looking for low-cal ways to satisfy your hunger can help you avoid taking in more calories than you just worked off. Exercise also increases the efficiency of insulin uptake in muscle cells—hampered when the EC system is overactive.

Exercise is the key to maintaining weight loss, because it counteracts the body's natural tendency to use fewer calories once you've lost weight, says Dr. Aronne. "The

Body chemistry can often be regulated through regular exercise. (AP Images)

body senses that less food is coming in, and its response is to conserve calories. What it does is makes your muscles more efficient, sort of like having a car that gets better milage as the gas gauge goes down. With a 10 percent reduction in body weight there's a 42 percent reduction in energy expended during physical activity. Exercise blunts that reduction in energy expenditure," he explains.

In the end, "there's no real shortcut to weight loss," concludes Dr. Aronne. "It amounts to taking in fewer calories and burning off more."

Thrifty Genes May Cause Obesity

Francine R. Kaufman

Francine R. Kaufman, a medical doctor, is a professor of pediatrics at the Keck School of Medicine of the University of Southern California. She is also a past president of the American Diabetes Association. In this selection from her book, *Diabesity*, she discusses how humans evolved from Paleolithic times to the present. She notes that our ancestors lived a physically active lifestyle as hunters and gatherers and had a diet that was low in fat and high in fiber. Because of their lifestyle, Kaufman says, they developed the ability to convert excess calories into fat to provide energy during lean times. These "thrifty genes" helped people survive then, but today contribute to the obesity epidemic.

About 40,000 years ago, on some savanna, a Paleolithic man and woman emerged to become the great, great, great . . . grandparents of us all. Their

SOURCE: Francine R. Kaufman, from *Diabesity: The Obesity-Diabetes Epidemic That Threatens America—And What We Must Do to Stop It*, New York, NY: Bantam Books, 2005. Copyright © 2005 by Francine Ratner Kaufman, M.D. All rights reserved. Used by permission of Bantam Books, a division of Random House, Inc., and the author.

Paleolithic genes still inhabit our cells; we continue to pass them from one generation to the next. And these genes shape our metabolic pathways. We must look to our Paleolithic ancestors to understand the modern-day problem of diabesity. We must look to them to know why the environment we have created is so toxic to our essential well-being. We must put ourselves in their place and in their lives to understand how the genes that must have been advantageous in the past are killing us now.

People Evolved Under Hardship Conditions

Our Paleolithic ancestors were hunters and gatherers. The men traveled long distances in search of food. They tracked wild creatures—predecessors of the bison, bear, and other large mammals that inhabit our earth now. They killed their prey with rocks and primitive spears. After the men feasted on the carcass, they hauled the remains home to feed their families. But sometimes the hunt was unsuccessful and they went hungry. In the presence of an unreliable food source, no one ever knew exactly when or where they would get the next meal. When food was present, especially the rarer and more precious fat and protein of animal products, gorging and trying to store calories within the body was a wise strategy.

Paleolithic men were lean, muscular, and strong. Their bodies evolved to withstand the perils that hid behind every tree and boulder in their ancient landscape. Between hunting, nomadic migration, and chasing off perilous intruders, they rarely had time to sit and relax. Their day was spent in vigorous physical activity. Insufficient food was a constant risk.

Women—the childbearers and nurturers—stayed closer to home. Like the men, they were physically active, but their work required more cunning than strength. They kept the fires burning and taught their young about danger and survival. To supplement whatever prizes the men brought back, the women foraged. They gathered nuts, berries, fruits, vegetables, and roots. Obesity was probably unheard of, because the food supply was so unreliable. But the women undoubtedly had a higher proportion of body fat than the men did, as is true for women today.

Our Ancestors Had a Varied Diet

Our Paleolithic ancestors enjoyed a varied diet. When the supply of game or vegetation ran low, the community moved to more promising land. Over the year, as seasons changed and they migrated in search of food and easier survival, they could consume up to a hundred dif-

Portion control is essential to maintaining a healthy weight. (AP Images)

ferent varieties of fruits, nuts, and vegetables. Children were nursed until age two or three. After weaning, their main beverage was water.

Our own dietary preferences reflect the needs of our Paleolithic ancestors. They could not have survived without receptivity to new foods; flexibility enhanced their ability to endure in changing environments. We share a built-in preference for variety. That's why we're more tempted to overeat at a buffet than when we're offered just a single option. Indeed, the success of some modern weight loss diets rests mainly upon the appetite-reducing effects of restricting food choices.

There is no doubt that our attraction to sweets is rooted in our genes. In Paleolithic times, plants with sweet fruit provided quick energy and were safe to eat. Since bitter plants were often poisonous, they were best avoided. Human taste evolved to prefer sweet foods because those were without peril in our ancient landscape.

We can't be certain, but our best guess is that the Paleolithic diet was approximately 30 percent protein. The chief protein sources were fish and meat. We can assume that the mammals our ancestors ate were lean. These beasts didn't live in feedlots or graze on carefully managed pastures. They had to exert themselves to obtain nourishment and to avoid becoming the meal of some other creature. So like the hunters who hunted them, they were largely muscle.

Paleolithic Diets Were High in Fiber

Probably about 50 percent of our ancestors' diet consisted of nuts, seeds, fruits, roots, and vegetables. Vitamins and minerals were abundant in these foods. Men and women consumed up to 100 grams of fiber per day—five to ten times as much as is typical today. About 20 percent of their diet was fat, mostly from nuts and seeds. The fat in nuts and seeds is the unsaturated kind, which actually helps keep blood vessels free of the damage that saturated fat can cause. Since the meat was lean, the Paleolithic diet included minimal saturated fat compared to today's diet.

Paleolithic men and women did not live long. If they survived birth and infancy, most died in what we would consider young adulthood. They were vulnerable to famine, predators, accidents, and infections; the women faced all this plus the risks of childbirth. But we can assume that our ancestors' health problems didn't include the obesity-related woes that plague us today. Their blood vessels presumably were free of fat deposits, so strokes, heart attacks, and high blood pressure were probably rare. Thanks to their high-fiber diet, their colons must have functioned well, without the modern woes of colon cancer and intestinal polyps, constipation, hemorrhoids, and fissures. Diabesity was unknown.

Thrifty Genes Helped People Survive

The genes that designed the bodies of our Paleolithic ancestors evolved for people who spent their days in physical activity and whose diet was low in calories and saturated fat. Evolution selected genes that could withstand a harsh reality: a tenuous food supply, barren winters, and recurrent droughts. In an influential article published in 1962, the late geneticist James Neel called them "thrifty" genes because they helped maximize the amount of energy that could be obtained and stored from every calorie consumed. One mechanism for accomplishing this was insulin resistance.

It's not hard to imagine how Paleolithic life selected who would live and who would die. Infant mortality was very high. In this harsh world, insulin resistance was an adaptive mechanism for babies, both before and after birth, enabling them to use meager calories more efficiently. In times when food was more plentiful, thrifty genes would enable them to eat heartily and stockpile body fat for the inevitable harder times. When famine came, thrifty genes would conserve those fat stores, slowing down metabolism and preserving the body's energy reserves as much as possible. Evolution favored those women able to accumulate body fat despite periods of famine, since they were more fertile and better able to endure the physical demands of pregnancy and nursing babies.

Thrifty genes were advantageous for Paleolithic life. But 5,000 to 10,000 years ago, much of the world began to change. Some bands of humans developed agriculture; others learned to domesticate animals. They abandoned their nomadic ways, settled down, and developed vast civilizations. These civilizations were able to grow crops rather than forage for them. They were able to raise animals in an enclosed space rather than hunt them. They were able to survive in larger groups because their food supply had become more reliable and they could store extra provisions. Famines and shortages, although not unheard of, became much less frequent. But there was a price to be paid for this progress. The balance that had evolved between humans and their nutritional environment was altered.

Thrifty Genes Are No Longer Important

With agriculture came a huge dietary shift: the preeminence of grain and increased consumption of meat. With abundant grain and food products developed from grain, humans consumed less fish, fruits, and vegetables. Animals raised for human consumption were fatter than the lean prey eaten by Paleolithic people, and the saturated fat they contained was less favorable to the human metabolic and cardiovascular systems.

Achim Gutersohn, a German geneticist, has hypothesized that the thrifty genes became less important in stable societies with better climates and more abundant food

> **FAST FACT**
>
> As of 2006 there are more people in the world who are overweight than are malnourished, according to the World Health Organization.

Weight Gain by Ethnic Group in the United States

Increase in Overweight and Obesity Prevalence Among U.S. Adults* by Racial/Ethnic Group

Racial / Ethnic Group	Overweight (BMI greater than 25) Prevalence percent		Obesity (BMI greater than 30) Prevalence percent	
	1988 to 1994	1999 to 2000	1988 to 1994	1999 to 2000
Black (non-Hispanic)	62.5	69.6	30.2	39.9
Mexican American	67.4	73.4	28.4	34.4
White (non-Hispanic)	52.6	62.3	21.2	28.7

*Ages 20 and older for 1999 to 2000 and ages 20 to 74 for 1988 to 1994.

Source: American Obesity Association. http://obesityusa.org/subs/fastfacts/Obesity_Minority_Pop.shtml.

supplies. His theory helps explain why diabesity is more common in some parts of the world than in others.

Thrifty genes are very common in Africans (and African Americans). Gutersohn estimates that 90 percent of those of African descent have thrifty genes. Since the food supply was not optimal in Africa, some of our ancient ancestors migrated to Eurasia. The food supply and climate were better in Eurasia, and the thrifty genes became less common in their descendants. Some settled in Asia, others in Europe. Perhaps 50 percent of Asians have thrifty genes, according to Gutersohn. But those who wound up in Europe made further improvements in food procurement. As the risk of starvation was reduced, more people who lacked genes to withstand famine could survive to adulthood and reproduce. That's why the thrifty genes are found in only 20 to 35 percent of Europeans and Americans descended from Europeans.

Meanwhile, in other corners of the globe, ancestors of the indigenous peoples of the Americas, Asia, the Pacific, and Africa continued to face a less-than-abundant food supply. Many still relied on hunting and gathering. Some farmed, but with less effective technology than that enjoyed by European farmers. Their thrifty genes remained important—and became all the more so when these peoples were conquered by a succession of European colonizers who decimated their lands, slaughtered their herds, and forced them to migrate across the planet under the most inhumane conditions imaginable.

number of people in the U.S.—is called *obesity*, or having an excessively high level of body fat.

What is the cause of the nation's expanding waistline? "Obesity is a very complex disease that involves many factors," explains Myles Faith, an obesity researcher at the University of Pennsylvania. So far, scientists have identified obesity-causing factors ranging from the way people eat to how they spend their pastimes to *genetics* (heredity). And with approximately 300,000 people dying from obesity-related complications each year, an all-time high, scientists are determined to help find solutions that will stop this disorder.

Defining Obesity

It takes more than a glance to determine if a person is obese. That's why scientists measure a person's *Body Mass Index* (BMI), a mathematical formula that calculates a person's weight adjusted for his or her height. If the BMI falls within a specified range, (25 to 29.9 kg/m2), an adult is considered overweight. For adults, if the BMI is above the overweight range (over 30 kg/m2), the adult is likely considered obese.

For people under the age of 20, scientists categorize the BMI differently. They use a chart of BMI ranges that's specific to the person's age and sex. And these ranges do not include a category for obesity. That's because growing boys accumulate fat differently from growing girls. Additionally, developing bodies have ever-changing fat levels. "So we talk in terms of 'underweight,' 'normal weight,' 'at risk of overweight,' and 'overweight,'" explains Michele Maynard, an *epidemiologist* (scientist who studies rates of diseases within a population) at the Centers for Disease Control and Prevention (CDC).

Scientists have found strong evidence that people who are overweight as kids and teens are likely to remain overweight or become obese in adulthood. Of particular concern: Since the 1980s, the number of overweight U.S.

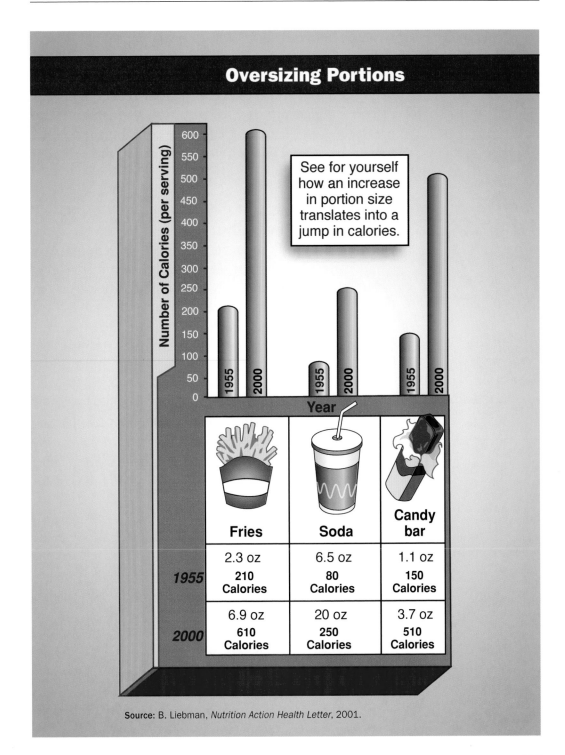

Oversizing Portions

See for yourself how an increase in portion size translates into a jump in calories.

Number of Calories (per serving)

	Fries	Soda	Candy bar
1955	2.3 oz **210** **Calories**	6.5 oz **80** **Calories**	1.1 oz **150** **Calories**
2000	6.9 oz **610** **Calories**	20 oz **250** **Calories**	3.7 oz **510** **Calories**

Source: B. Liebman, *Nutrition Action Health Letter*, 2001.

children between ages 2 and 11 has more than doubled. Even more staggering: In adolescents between ages 12 and 19, the number has more than tripled. "We've also been seeing children and adolescents with increased frequency of *type 2 diabetes* (blood-sugar disorder) and high blood pressure," says Maynard. "These are conditions once primarily associated with adults." Why are so many bodies now tipping the scales?

Big Questions

Like a machine, the body needs fuel to operate. When you eat, your body converts that food into energy. And what your body does not use for fuel is stored as reserve —fat. "Obesity is caused by an imbalance between energy input and energy output," says Maynard. That means, when anyone consumes more *calories* (energy units in food) than he or she is able to use, or *expend*, the body is likely to gain fat.

But every person's *metabolism* (chemical reactions in the body that change food into energy) is different. And the mystery of why some people tend to pack on fat easier than others has led scientists to search for clues. "We believe that *genes* (units of hereditary information) play a major role in obesity," says Shirly Pinto, a biologist at Rockefeller University.

Scientists Find Weight-Controlling Hormone

In 1994, scientists at Rockefeller University made a breakthrough: They discovered that fat cells produce an appetite-controlling hormone (function-controlling chemical), which they named *leptin*. This hormone keeps people at a healthy weight. It signals a brain region responsible for maintaining weight levels—the *hypothalamus*—information on how much fuel the body needs. In other words, leptin sends out the "I'm full" message. When you have fewer fat cells, less leptin is produced, signaling you to eat more. And with more fat cells, leptin levels increase, signaling you to eat less.

How does leptin relate to obesity? "In most cases, obese individuals have leptin levels that are higher than normal," says Pinto. "In a sense, they should stop eating. But they don't." Scientists believe that some obese people may have genetic differences that cause their bodies to be resistant to leptin's messages.

Since leptin's discovery, scientists have found other hormones that are involved in how the body perceives food. Could hormone-regulating, fat-fighting medicines result soon? It's too early to tell. How these natural hormones work alone—much less, how they interact with each other—is still unclear. "Scientists are just starting to piece this puzzle together," says Pinto.

Even if some people have genes that make them more susceptible to becoming obese, that does not fully explain why the number of obese Americans has recently sky-rocketed. Scientists point to today's lifestyles as a big part of the problem.

Modern Problems

"Americans live in an environment that favors a sedentary lifestyle and an over consumption of food," says Maynard. And technological advances are partly to blame. Today, from transportation to entertainment to work tools, "we desire what's convenient," says Faith. "We have cars, TV, the computer—but they are major reasons why Americans lead such an inactive lifestyle." For example, according to the U.S. Department of Health and Human Services, one quarter of U.S. children between ages 8 and 16 spend at least four hours a day watching TV.

To control weight and fat levels, the CDC recommends that teens perform at least one hour of moderately intense physical activity every day. "Short bouts of various

FAST FACT

Obesity in the U.S. population has risen by 61 percent over ten years (1991 to 2000).

activities count toward meeting this recommendation. Even raking the lawn or taking the stairs require you to expend energy," says Maynard.

A sedentary lifestyle is made unhealthier by poor food choices. Today, people consume a lot of pre-packaged and "fast" foods, which tend to be high in fat and calories. And portion sizes have increased over the years. Maynard suggests that teens learn about appropriate serving sizes and replace high-caloric snacks with fruits and vegetables.

By overcoming obesity, people would reap colossal medical and social benefits.

Obesity Is Not
a Disease

Paul Ernsberger

Paul Ernsberger is a professor in the Department of Nutrition at Case Western Reserve University School of Medicine. In this viewpoint he argues that obesity does offer some health benefits. He cites research from multiple studies that indicate that the cancer mortality rate is lower when an individual is fatter. He also documents that increased body mass index (BMI) is correlated with lower death rates from diseases such as emphysema, bronchitis, pneumonia, and tuberculosis. Increased fat leads to increased bone mass, Ernsberger notes. Some cardiovascular diseases also have a lower occurrence among people with a higher BMI. Ernsberger concludes that obesity cannot be considered a disease because of the health benefits that the condition offers.

Is obesity a disease? This question is currently debated within science and medicine. Historically, body size has been considered a risk factor for disease rather than a true disorder. Body weight was one of many

SOURCE: Paul Ernsberger, "Health Benefits of Obesity," *Health at Every Size*, Winter 2007, pp. 185–93. Reproduced by permission.

potential risk factors considered in postwar longitudinal trials, such as the Framingham and Seven Countries studies. Obesity is usually treated as [a] secondary risk factor, meaning that its negative associations arise from its associations with primary risk factors such as blood pressure, blood sugar and cholesterol. Recently, some weight loss advocates have advanced the idea that obesity is a true disease. The acceptance of obesity as a disease has diverse consequences. Notably, if obesity is a disease then weight loss programs represent disease treatments and as such must be fully covered by health insurance. Massive expansion of the weight loss medicoindustrial complex would be the necessary result.

An obvious property of diseases is that they do not have beneficial effects. Diseases lead to adverse consequences, not to a mix of positive and negative outcomes. Here we review the evidence that obesity has health benefits. . . . An independent review of the health benefits of adipose tissue has appeared, with a focus on benefits to reproductive, bone and immune system health. The present essay does not imply that the beneficial associations of obesity outweigh its harmful associations—they almost definitely do not. However, the impact of obesity on an individual may include both positive and negative influences on health. Because the positive effects have been almost entirely neglected, this article will focus on these exclusively.

Fat Reduces Cancer Death Rates

The fatter an individual is, the less likely they are to die of cancer during subsequent years. As of 1987, this had been shown in at least seven studies, most notably in the [1985] multinational Seven Countries Study. In all of these studies, the protective effect of high body weight was not emphasized or mentioned in the abstract, but was only mentioned in the data tables. More recent epidemiological studies have mostly reported neutral find-

Social influences may play an important role in the development of childhood obesity.
(AP Images)

ings. For example, in the 25-year follow up of the White-hall study from the U.K., cancer deaths were 0.77% per year in people with a normal BMI, 0.75% for being over-weight and 0.79% for the obese.

Considerable publicity was given to a questionnaire study, sponsored by the American Cancer Society, with 1.1 million participants. Over three-quarters of the sub-jects were excluded, however, primarily if they had ever been exposed to tobacco smoke. In the remaining group, increased cancer risk was only found in the very fattest of the subjects, those having a BMI over 40. Among the men, "overweight" was slightly protective. For women, almost all of the risk could be explained by a higher rate of uter-ine cancer, which is largely preventable with appropriate gynecological care. No consideration was given the socioeconomic effects. Poverty is associated with obesity and also with exposure to environmental pollutants, including carcinogens. All of the older studies that found a protective effect of obesity used defined cohorts that were similar in social status or city of residence.

The relationship of body weight to cancers at specific locations is complex and studies tend to be contradictory. One consistent finding has been the protective effect of obesity on breast cancer in pre-menopausal women. After menopause and especially after age 65, obesity is associated with a higher risk of breast cancer. Breast cancer is more likely to be lethal when it occurs at a young age, and leads to many more lost years of potential life. Thus, the overall effect of obesity on years of life lost to breast cancer is probably most beneficial for pre-menopausal women.

There are a number of reports that cancer patients have better survival if they are lean. However, quality of health care is a major factor influencing survival, as is the timing of cancer diagnosis. Many fat people avoid physician visits or lack health insurance. Several studies have shown that the fatter a patient is, the less likely they are to be offered cancer screening tests. Medical bias against fat patients can have lethal results if cancer goes undetected.

Rising BMI Decreases Respiratory Deaths

The death rate for common lung diseases such as emphysema, bronchitis and pneumonia decreases with increasing BMI. This correlation is partially caused by weight loss during the progression of lung diseases. However, there is also strong evidence that obesity has protective effects. The association between low body weight and lung dysfunction is found as early as adolescence. Obese lung patients (those with a BMI greater than 30) show a slower rate of disease progression than thinner patients. Obese lung injury patients are more likely to survive than lean patients. Most importantly, interventions to promote weight gain improve survival in chronic lung disease. It is possible that many lives could be saved if weight gain programs were instituted for lung disease patients. Sadly, despite evidence from clinical trials, weight gain therapy is not likely to be implemented.

Overall mortality from infectious disease, especially pneumonia and tuberculosis, declines with increasing body weight. More recently, it has been confirmed that the higher a person's BMI at the time of diagnosis of HIV infection, the greater their chances for survival.

Bone Diseases Decline with Obesity

Possibly the clearest beneficial effect of obesity is on bone health. Bone mass rises in direct proportion to BMI. The fatter you are the less your risk of osteoporosis. Osteoporosis is not only painful and potentially disabling, but can also lead to death, most commonly by contributing to hip fracture. Obesity also protects against the risk of bone fracture in rheumatoid arthritis.

Why does increased fat mass lead to increased bone mass? There may be a causal connection through the hormone estrogen. Fat cells have the ability to create estrogen-like hormones from adrenal hormones. As a result, the fatter a person is the higher their level of estrogen. While estrogen can have harmful effects in terms of uterine cancer and postmenopausal breast cancer, it has beneficial effects which can be seen in fat people. Estrogen acts on cells residing in our bones to increase the formation of new bone and reduce the leaching of calcium out of bones.

Scoliosis is strongly related to low BMI in adolescents, and a cause and effect relationship between undernutrition and spinal malformation is considered likely.

Prevalence of Obesity in the United States

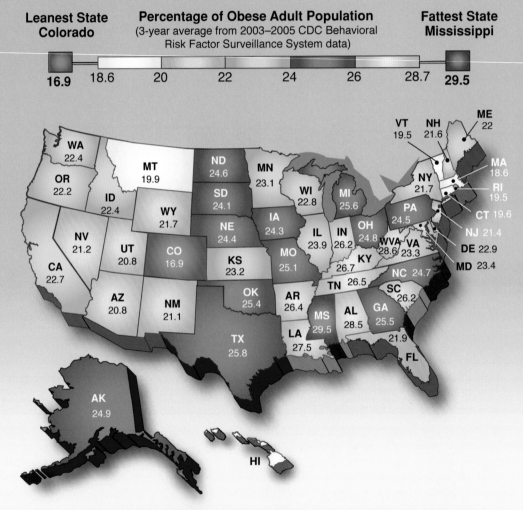

Leanest State
Colorado

Percentage of Obese Adult Population
(3-year average from 2003–2005 CDC Behavioral
Risk Factor Surveillance System data)

Fattest State
Mississippi

16.9   18.6   20   22   24   26   28.7   29.5

ME 22
VT 19.5   NH 21.6
WA 22.4
MT 19.9
ND 24.6
MN 23.1
NY 21.7
MA 18.6
RI 19.5
OR 22.2
ID 22.4
WY 21.7
SD 24.1
WI 22.8
MI 25.6
PA 24.5
CT 19.6
NV 21.2
UT 20.8
CO 16.9
NE 24.4
IA 24.3
IL 23.9
IN 26.2
OH 24.8
WV 28.6
VA 23.3
NJ 21.4
DE 22.9
CA 22.7
KS 23.2
MO 25.1
KY 26.7
MD 23.4
AZ 20.8
NM 21.1
OK 25.4
AR 26.4
TN 26.5
NC 24.7
SC 26.2
MS 29.5
AL 28.5
GA 25.5
TX 25.8
LA 27.5
FL 21.9
AK 24.9
HI

(Data not collected for Hawaii in 2004; average of 2003 and 2005 is 18.1.)

Source: Carleton College: Carleton Lifestyles Program. http://apps.carleton.edu/
MindBodySpirit/lifestyles/assets/US_obesity.jpg.

Larger Mothers Have Fewer Low Birth Weight Babies

The fatter the mother, the larger the newborn. Because low birth weight is a much more significant problem for the future life of the child, high weight during pregnancy is more beneficial than harmful to the offspring. Very large infants pose risks to the mother during birth, and risks to the fetus can occur if pregnancy continues too long past the due date. This is usually addressed by inducing labor or scheduling a cesarean section. Fatter mothers are more likely to require cesarean delivery. In one study, mothers weighing over 300 pounds were found to have more complications, mainly cesarean delivery and having large babies. However, even these complications were entirely due to some women having high blood pressure or diabetes prior to pregnancy. Women weighing over 300 pounds who had normal blood pressures and blood sugars had no increase in complications.

> **FAST FACT**
>
> A U.S. Circuit Court of Appeals ruled that a 405-pound worker was not disabled as defined by the Americans with Disability Act because his weight was not related to a physiological problem.

Either very high or very low body weight can result in infertility. High body weight leads to irregular menstrual cycles because of high levels of estrogen, which can be countered by progesterone treatment. Low body weight and excessive dieting may be a major cause of infertility. We now know that low levels of leptin, as a result of insufficient adipose tissue, are the cause of infertility in lean women.

Some Heart Diseases Are Associated with Low BMIs

Mitral valve prolapse is associated with low BMI. More recent studies confirm this finding especially in adolescents. Recent studies have also identified cardiovascular abnormalities in anorexia, a disease which is diagnosed in part on the basis of a BMI below 18.5. Anorexic patients have a very high risk of mitral valve abnormalities, as might be predicted from their low BMI, and also show pericardial effusions, which is the accumulation of fluid under the protective membrane that surrounds the heart. These abnormalities may contribute to the high risk of sudden cardiac death in anorexia. Whether or not such abnormalities might contribute to disease or death in very thin women who are not anorexic remains to be determined.

Mitral valve regurgitation is also more common in those with low BMI. This is significant, because this condition has been linked to the use of diet pills such as dexfenfluramine and fen-phen. Pharmaceutical firms defending against liability lawsuits have claimed that obesity, not diet pills, was the cause of mitral valve regurgitation. The data show the opposite, that obesity is actually protective. . . .

Recent studies have shown that this disease [peripheral vascular disease], caused by hardening of the arteries in the legs, is for the most part unrelated to BMI or related positively in women but not in men. Obesity is probably not protective against this disease. . . .

Conclusions

Obesity is associated with a lower risk of a number of serious diseases. In terms of the number of deaths, protection against death from cancer, lung diseases, and bone fractures due to osteoporosis are probably the most important, followed by protection against infectious diseases and suicide. These protective effects probably explain why the relationship between BMI and the risk of death takes a U shape, with increased risk at both the low and the high end of the weight spectrum. The conditions described in this review can help explain the left side of the U corresponding to high risks with low BMI. Other conditions reviewed in this essay also contribute substantially to disability, especially during adolescence for women and during old age for both genders.

Correlation does not equal causation. We do not know if obesity directly gives rise to these protective effects, or whether high body weight is only an "innocent bystander" to these health benefits. Some of the beneficial effects could plausibly be caused by increased levels of estrogens produced by adipose tissue. Estrogens have protective effects on bones, the circulation, and on the brain to prevent mood disorders that can lead to suicide. Beneficial effects on bones can also arise from mechanical effects of increased weight, because the mechanical effects of bearing more weight can help maintain bone mass. Beyond these plausible explanations, there is little that is known. Compared to the vast efforts expended to chart the health risks of obesity, almost nothing is known about the very real health risks of leanness.

Perhaps the most important conclusion is that obesity cannot be considered a disease. Diseases do not have health benefits. Diseases are not associated with improved prognosis in other diseases. Obese people with high blood pressure, congestive heart failure, type 2 diabetes, and high cholesterol all have better outcomes than lean people with these same conditions. Thus, even if the net impact of obesity on health is negative because its hazards exceed its benefits, it can only be considered a condition or at most a risk factor, but certainly not a true disease in its own right.

Gastric Bypass Surgery Offers Hope to the Obese

Tracy Connor

Tracy Connor is a staff writer for the *New York Daily News*. In this viewpoint Connor demonstrates the benefits of gastric surgery for the severely obese using the publicized examples of celebrities' surgeries. The *Today* show's Al Roker, singer Ann Wilson, and actor Michael Genadry have all had surgery to drop more than one hundred pounds. Doctors note that celebrities have set the examples for the public to follow, and the prevalence of gastric operations is rapidly increasing. Connor also highlights the success of surgery for the average person to drop the weight and alleviate health problems.

Al Roker's idea of a snack used to be half a dozen Krispy Kreme doughnuts, but he just doesn't have the stomach for it anymore.

The *Today* show weatherman has joined a parade of corpulent celebrities taking a radical step to slim down: gastric surgery.

SOURCE: Tracy Connor, "Celebrities Put Fat-Fighting Surgery in the Spotlight," *New York Daily News*, November 17, 2002. Copyright © 2002 New York Daily News, L.P. Reprinted with permission.

After years of yo-yo dieting, Roker had his stomach stapled and his small intestine rerouted so that he can only eat a few ounces of food at a time.

Eight months later, he has dropped 100 pounds from his 320-pound frame, trimmed 14 inches from his waist and put all those Fat Albert jokes to rest.

"The weight just started dropping like water," Roker, 48, said as he showed off his new silhouette on the cover of *People* magazine earlier this month [November 2002].

Surgery for Celebrities

He's not the only incredible shrinking star.

Pop singer Carnie Wilson lost 150 pounds after surgery. Heavy-metal mama Sharon Osbourne went from 225 pounds to 130 in nine months.

Rep. Jerrold Nadler, reportedly down 61 pounds since August [2002], Blues Traveler frontman John Popper and Heart rocker Ann Wilson have also gone under the knife.

"I'm down about 60 pounds—I have another 50 or 60 pounds to go," reported Ann Wilson, who had a restrictive band placed around her stomach last January [2002] and is now paid to promote the procedure.

Actor Michael Genadry, who plays a high school student on the NBC sitcom *Ed*, was 461 pounds when he had the operation in September [2002]. He has dropped nearly 70 pounds. "I used to be able to eat an entire 18-inch pizza pie in one sitting," he said.

"Now I've just gotten to the point where I can eat an entire slice. But it takes me an hour or more to finish it."

Many Follow Celebrities' Examples

Genadry, 24, first heard of the surgery when Carnie Wilson went public with her operation in 2001.

"It's gotten extremely popular as a result of celebrities," said Dr. George Angus, director of bariatric medicine at Nassau University Medical Center. In 1992, there were an estimated 16,000 of the fat-fighting operations

Ann Wilson, lead singer for the band Heart, chose the Lap-Band method for her gastric surgery. (AP Images)

performed in the United States. This year [2002], some 63,000 people will get the surgery, the American Society of Bariatric Surgeons said.

Medical experts are quick to warn that the procedure is a last resort only for the morbidly obese, a major operation that carries a 1-in-200 risk of death. Doctors will only operate on people at least 100 pounds overweight who have tried aggressive dieting programs and failed.

The Procedures

There are two basic surgeries.

The one approved just last year [2001] is known as the Lap-Band. An adjustable silicone belt is wrapped around the upper stomach. The restriction makes patients —Ann Wilson and Osbourne among them—feel full faster, forcing them to eat less.

The more popular operation is gastric bypass. It has been around since 1967 and can help patients lose much more weight than the band, doctors said.

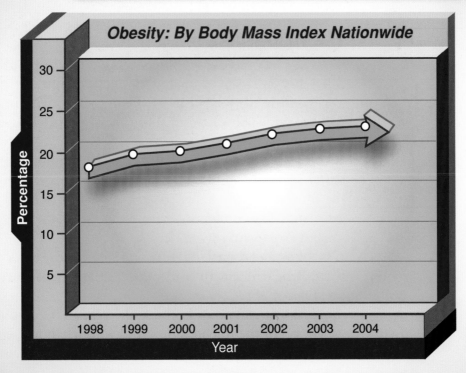

The Rise in Obesity

BRFSS (Behavioral Risk Factor Surveillance System) data shows that in 1998, 18.3 percent of the population was obese; by 2004, it was 23.2 percent.

Obesity: By Body Mass Index Nationwide

Source: Behavioral Risk Factor Surveillance System. "Trends in Obesity," March 9, 2006. www.cdc.gov/brfss/training/interviewer/01_section/08_trends_obesity.htm.

Surgeons staple the stomach into two compartments and connect a piece of the small intestine to the upper portion, which becomes the working stomach.

Since the pouch is roughly the size of an egg, the patient can eat only tiny amounts of food—a few tablespoons at first, up to 5 ounces after a year.

Taking in too much is painful. And because not all the food is absorbed, patients must take vitamins, iron and calcium pills for the rest of their lives.

"It's important to realize this is major surgery," said Dr. Daniel Herron, of Mount Sinai Medical Center.

"That said, you have to compare the risk from surgery to the risk of being overweight." He said the severely obese are two or three times more likely than the average person to die from a health problem—and their quality of life can be dire.

The Operations Work

Genadry was having trouble sleeping, migraine headaches, hip and joint aches and lower back pain.

"Food used to be kind of the major priority in my life," he said. "Now I think about food so little I have to remind myself to eat."

Not every surgery is a success story. Some patients suffer serious complications. Others never get used to the food restrictions, fail to exercise or continue to indulge in forbidden foods.

But the operations work.

Angus had a patient who, at 430 pounds, was confined to a wheelchair and needed a tracheostomy to breathe.

"She lost 250 pounds," he said. "Within two months we got rid of the tracheostomy and wheelchair and eight months later, I couldn't recognize her."

Gastric Bypass Surgery Poses Medical Risks

Ben Harder

Author Ben Harder is a regular contributor to *Science News*. In the following viewpoint he examines the complications that can arise from gastric bypass surgery. He notes that while the surgery can alleviate a number of conditions, including type 2 diabetes, sleep apnea, high cholesterol, and high blood pressure, the surgery does carry risks. Harder notes that hospitalization rates increase for people who have had the surgery. In addition to the higher rates of hospitalization, Harder cites research that shows that death rates among surgery recipients are higher than those of the general population. Recognizing that the surgery is the best solution for some, the authorities Harder cites call for caution in evaluating the risks.

Obese people who opt for weight-loss surgery incur increased odds of subsequent hospitalization and, in some groups, a substantial risk of death, say researchers who have investigated this burgeoning

SOURCE: Ben Harder, "Weight-Loss Costs," *Science News*, vol. 168, October 22, 2005, pp. 260–61. Reprinted with permission from *Science News*, the weekly newsmagazine of science. Copyright © 2005 by Science Service.

FAST FACT

Statistics show that one in three hundred gastric bypass patients die from the surgery.

treatment. Even so, some of the scientists say, those risks may be justified.

Gastric-bypass surgery—which detours food around most of the stomach—and other weight-loss, or bariatric, operations usually mitigate numerous conditions, including diabetes, sleep apnea, and high blood pressure and cholesterol. Nationwide, surgery is an option for about 10 million severely obese people, says David R. Flum of the University of Washington in Seattle.

Five times as many women as men choose a weight-loss operation, usually after dieting and exercise fail, according to an analysis of hospital records by Heena P. Santry of the University of Chicago and her colleagues. They found that the surgical patients are primarily people from wealthy communities and who have private insurance.

Santry's team estimates that doctors performed 102,794 bariatric operations in 2003, up from 13,365 in 1998. More than 80 percent of the procedures were gastric bypasses.

Rates of immediate deaths and complications from weight-loss surgery stayed even during the years investigated, but average recovery time in the hospital decreased from 4.5 to 3.3 days, Santry's team reports in the Oct. 19 *Journal of the American Medical Association* (JAMA).

Gastric Bypass Surgery Carries Risks

The operations nevertheless have substantial risks. David S. Zingmond of the University of California, Los Angeles and two colleagues found signs that gastric bypass increased the risk of serious health problems for several years. For example, 19.3 percent of California patients who had undergone the surgery returned to a hospital within a year. By comparison, only 7.9 percent had been hospitalized in the year before the surgery.

Hospitalization rates hovered around 15 percent or higher during the second and third years after gastric bypass, Zingmond's team reports in the same JAMA issue. Costs associated with the 3-year increase in hospitalization could amount to roughly half again the $25,000 price tag for the surgery, the researchers say.

Such costs might have already dissuaded insurance companies from readily sponsoring weight-loss operations for some patients, Zingmond says. Gastric-bypass operations in California peaked in 2003, before declining by nearly 15 percent in 2004, he notes.

Medicare Patients Have Higher Risks

In a third report in JAMA, Flum and other Seattle-based investigators examined [the] surgery's risks among bariatric patients who receive Medicare. Those patients, who

The risk of infection during surgery can be a detrimental side effect of gastric bypass surgery. (AP Images)

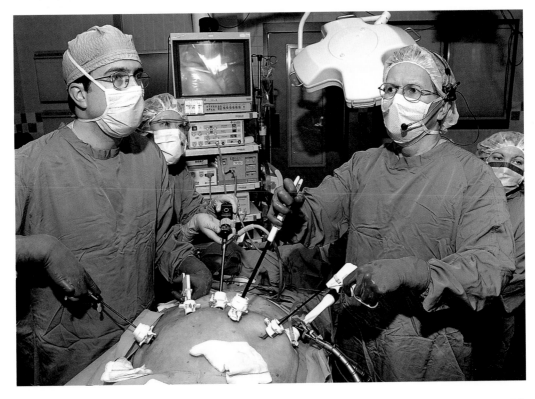

account for about 6 percent of bariatric surgeries nation-wide, tend to be disabled by their obesity, Flum says. This might give them more to gain by surgery.

The researchers found that 2 percent of Medicare patients died within a month of surgery and 4.6 percent died within a year. Those death rates exceed comparable values for elective coronary-bypass and hip-replacement operations as well as rates in past studies of bariatric operations that were performed by well-practiced surgeons on select patients.

Among the Medicare patients, those who were male, older than 65 years, or had the surgery performed by teams with limited experience in bariatric procedures had the highest risk of dying in the first 3 months or year after surgery, Flum's team found.

"It's not that we shouldn't do the operation," says Flum. "It's the only intervention that provides significant and sustained weight loss for obese individuals." But patients, doctors, and institutions that pay for health care, he says, must consider the risks in deciding who should receive an operation and where.

Schools Must Help Fight Obesity

Glenn Cook

The following article is written by Glenn Cook, the editor in chief of *American School Board Journal*. In it, Cook discusses the role schools play in attempting to stop the dramatic rise in childhood obesity. The author notes that school districts across the country are beginning to include the body mass index (BMI) along with academic grades on students' report cards. The author points out that the progress in tackling obesity varies from state to state.

Walk into any fast-food restaurant these days and you are confronted with a host of healthy choice alternatives, a sign that the "Super Size Me" era is finally coming to an end. But how are efforts to curtail childhood obesity coming along, and what are the dangers and risks ahead?

SOURCE: Glenn Cook, "Childhood Obesity Battle Faces Hurdles, Hiccups," *American School Board Journal*, March, 2007, pp. 2–3. Copyright 2007 by the National School Boards Association. All rights reserved. Reprinted with permission from *American School Board Journal*.

It depends on whom you ask. But based on the flurry of reports and news articles during a one-week period in January [2007], it's obvious schools remain at the center of the food chain. And that comes as no surprise, given that about 17 percent of U.S. youngsters are obese and millions more are overweight.

Here are some things to consider when people ask you about schools and your efforts to curb childhood obesity.

BMI Bandwagon and Backlash

More states are focusing on reporting students' body mass index (BMI) scores to parents, turning the process into what the *New York Times* calls "a new rite of childhood."

Arkansas, Delaware, Pennsylvania, South Carolina, and Tennessee are being joined by other states in adding obesity grades to student report cards. In Virginia, legislation has been proposed that would require a BMI measurement for every first-time kindergarten or elementary school student.

A number of local school districts are adding BMI or personalized fitness reports to report cards as well, prompting some health officials to worry about the long-term effects on students, such as eating disorders and social stigmas.

"It would be the height of irony if we successfully identified overweight kids through BMI screening and notification while continuing to feed them atrocious quality meals and snacks, with limited if any opportunities for phys ed in school," Dr. David Ludwig, director of Optimal Weight for Life program at Children's Hospital Boston, told the *Times*.

The Centers for Disease Control and Prevention has been working on a policy statement on BMI reports for schools that will provide some guidelines on their benefits and risks. The statement had not been released at press time.

Progress at the State Level

Despite progress in a number of districts, many schools continue to serve junk food in their cafeterias. One state that will not: New Jersey, where legislators put the finishing touches on a law that requires schools to ban candy, snacks, soda, and high-fat junk food from their cafeterias

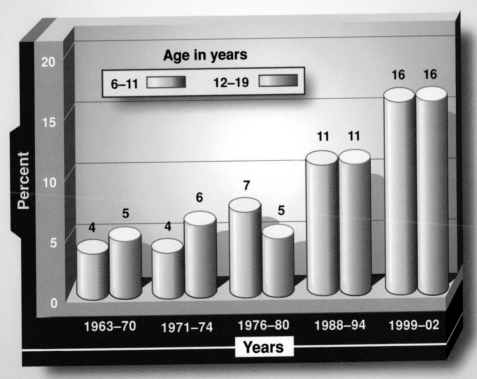

Prevalence of Overweight Children and Adolescents Ages 6–19 Years

Source: AtlantiCare. www.atlanticare.org.

and vending machines. Schools must make the changes by September [2007].

Eleven states, including Alabama, Arkansas, and Tennessee, have raised the nutritional standards for their schools' meals programs. Other states, such as Mississippi, have adopted new policies to curb the sales of low-nutrition snacks and soda in schools.

Seventeen states now have "snack taxes" to discourage all purchases of fatty and sugar-added snacks and drinks. And while every state except South Dakota has some physical education requirements, 47 states now require health education.

One state that is not getting a good grade in the obesity fight is California. Children Now, an Oakland-based group that grades the state on health, education, and the condition of families, said the state is largely failing to combat obesity. According to the report, about one in three children is overweight or obese. Among low-income children, the number increases to 37 percent.

The D-plus grade came even though Gov. Arnold Schwarzenegger has signed off on a plan to provide $40 million for more P.E. teachers and $500 million in one-time funding for schools to purchase sports equipment.

What Researchers Are Saying

It's not easy being a tween, especially if you are a girl, according to a report in the January [2007] *Journal of Pediatrics*. According to the report, girls ages 9 to 12 are at a higher risk of becoming overweight than when they are teenagers. Health risks include increased blood pressure, cholesterol, and diabetes.

Dr. Denise Simons-Morton, who heads obesity-prevention efforts at the National Institutes of Health's National Heart, Lung, and Blood Institute, called the age group "particularly vulnerable."

In October, the National Health and Nutrition Examination Survey said about one-third of U.S. adoles-

Educational programs such as *Sesame Street* can help promote healthy eating. **(AP Images)**

cents are out of shape and likely cannot pass a basic cardiovascular fitness test.

In December the *Pediatrics* journal also published a study which said children are gaining too much weight because they don't exercise enough and overeat by as much as 165 calories a day. The study by the Harvard School of Public Health examined weight gain in teens to develop what they call an "energy gap." One startling statistic: Obese children—averaging 58 pounds overweight—eat 700 to 1,000 calories more daily than they would need if they maintained a healthful weight.

Harvard sociologist Steven Gortmaker, who conducted the study, said obese children get about 350 calories daily from sugary beverages such as soda and juices.

Think about that last fact the next time you reach for a soda.

Schools' Attempts to Reduce Obesity Are Controversial

Anne Marie Chaker

In the following article Anne Marie Chaker details the backlash that one school district is experiencing for its efforts to combat childhood obesity. Chaker highlights the experience of Gillette, Wyoming, in attempting to curb the problem. She describes how parents react when they are told that their children are obese. Chaker tells how Gillette schools established a task force to help control obesity rates. As a result of this initiative, school cafeterias are restricting second helpings to fruit and vegetables, a health and nutrition program has been established, and teachers are getting bonuses for controlling their own weight. Many students and their parents rebel against school-sponsored programs such as these, Chaker says. In some schools the body mass index (BMI) has become an optional feature of the report card. While raising awareness, these programs also bring denial, hurt feelings, and resentment.

SOURCE: Anne Marie Chaker, "In Obesity Wars, a New Backlash," *The Wall Street Journal,* April 14, 2007, pp. A1, A4. Republished with permission of *The Wall Street Journal,* conveyed through Copyright Clearance Center, Inc.

Brittany Burns, 12 years old, has always been on the heavy side. Last year [2006] in fifth grade, neighborhood kids started picking on her at the bus stop, calling her "fatty" and "chubby wubby." Then someone else piled on: Brittany's school.

In a letter dated Oct. 2, 2006, the Campbell County School District No. 1 invited "select students" to take part in a fitness and nutrition program set up for some of the district's most overweight kids. At 5 feet 2 inches tall and 179 pounds, Brittany qualified.

Receiving the letter was "embarrassing," Brittany says. Her mother, Mindi Story, a clerk at an Albertsons supermarket, says she seethed "pure anger" because, she argues, her daughter's weight shouldn't be the school's concern: "I send her to school to learn math and reading."

School Offensive Against Obesity

Spurred by a local doctor and an enthusiastic school board, Gillette has banned soda and second helpings on hot meals. This year, it included students' body-mass index—a number that measures weight adjusted for height—on report cards, and started recommending students like Brittany for after-school fitness programs. It even offers teachers the chance to earn bonuses based on their fitness.

While the extent of Gillette's weight campaign makes it an outlier, the school district is just one of many communities stepping up efforts to tackle childhood obesity. At the Buckeye Central Local School District in New Washington, Ohio, officials have replaced large cookies with smaller ones. Stewart Middle School in Norristown, Pa., has limited the number of snacks students can buy to one a day. Burning Tree Elementary School in Bethesda, Md., now asks parents to bring fruit and juice for class parties instead of chips and soda.

Arkansas, Pennsylvania and a few other states require that students' body-mass index be recorded and sent home to parents periodically. Starting this school year [2007], a new federal rule requires that all school districts receiving meal subsidies create a "wellness policy" outlining goals for nutrition and fitness.

New Rules Spark Backlash

Schools like this one in Pittsburgh have begun using weight-loss tools like Z Trim, a fat replacement substance. (**AP Images**)

Many health experts approve, given how much time children spend at school. Schools create "social norms," says Marlene Schwartz, Director of Research and School Programs at Yale University's Rudd Center for Food Policy and Obesity. "The school is the perfect place to both teach things intellectually, but also create an environment where those lessons are reinforced."

But across the country, the new rules are also sparking a backlash among parents, children and even some teachers and school officials. The efforts often draw derision for being too extreme and demonizing children. Arkansas, the first state to pass legislation requiring schools to measure students' body-mass index, backtracked last month and now allows parents to refuse the assessment. The question of weight in Arkansas has been a sensitive one since former Gov. Mike Huckabee shed more than 100 pounds a few years ago and encouraged locals to follow his example. . . .

One Town Tackles Obesity

Gillette is a dusty, bustling coal-mining center in northeastern Wyoming, bisected by a railroad operated by Burlington Northern Santa Fe Corp., which delivers coal to such cities as Chicago and Centralia, Wash. Against empty sky, a water tower proclaims the city the "Energy Capital of the Nation." . . .

About three years ago, for the first time in his nearly 20 years as a doctor in the area, school board chairman and local pediatrician David Fall started seeing cases of overweight children with diabetes. An informal survey of patients suggested that about 15% were overweight, close to the national average. Those who were overweight, he noticed, were "way overweight." At the school board, he says, "we decided this was an issue we should look into."

Across the U.S., about 17% of children and adolescents age two to 19 are overweight, more than triple the percentage of 30 years ago, according to the federal Centers for Disease Control and Prevention. The CDC defines overweight children as those with a body-mass index in the 95th percentile and above, which puts them at increased risk for chronic health problems such as hypertension, certain types of diabetes and heart disease.

In 2004, Dr. Fall organized the Healthy Schools Task Force and recruited about two dozen parents and teachers.

First item on the list: Removing soda machines from schools in the district. "The biggest grief we got was from the teachers," Dr. Fall recalls, because schools also took machines out of teachers' lounges. "Some of them are still mad at me. They called me the 'Pop Nazi.'"

The task force decided students would no longer receive second-helpings of lunch entrées (they could have unlimited helpings of fresh fruits, vegetables and salad). It told lunch servers to give smaller portions to younger students. Concession-stand vendors received a list of recommended alternatives, such as fresh fruit and string cheese. School principals were pushed to dump bake sales in favor of car washes, talent shows and walkathons.

The task force also deployed financial incentives. Elementary schools that added physical activity received extra funding for instructors and after-school health programs. Based on the assumption that children emulate adults around them, the district in February began awarding bonuses to faculty who opted to receive a fitness assessment, which measured metrics such as blood pressure and bicep strength. The better the fitness score, the higher the bonus—as much as $160 if they take the test twice a year and get high marks.

Backlash Against the Task Force

Toward the end of 2004, parents started complaining at task-force meetings that their children were coming home hungry. One parent criticized the group for making unilateral decisions without involving the community.

"My kids are in every sport there is," says parent Mary Lou Gladson, who attended one of the meetings. "But they aren't big fruit and vegetable eaters. My kids were getting the short end of the stick because of the obese kids."

Even determining who is overweight has proven nettlesome. Nine-year-old Jeremy Holwell, who attends Lakeview Elementary, swims in a local league several nights a week and plays baseball in the summer. Gestur-

Funding and Disease Prevalence Comparisons in the United States

	National Institute of Health Funding	Prevalence
AIDS	$2.9 billion dollars	566 thousand adults
Cardiovascular Disease	$2.4 billion dollars	64 million adults
Diabetes	$1.1 billion dollars	18 million adults
Smoking	$566 million dollars	46 million adults
Obesity	$440 million dollars	64 million adults

 = $200 million dollars   ¢ = $100 million dollars   = 10 million adults

Source: NIH Estimates of Funding for Various Diseases, Conditions, Research Areas. HIV AIDS Surveillance Report, Vol. 15, 2003, Table 12. Estimated Number of Adults/Adolescents Living with HIV Infection or AIDS. American Heart Association's "Heart Disease & Stroke Statistics - 2004 Update." American Diabetes Association Online. Diabetes Statistics (www.diabetes.org/diabetes-statistics.jsp). CDC Tobacco Information & Prevention Source, "Cigarette Smoking Among Adults–United States, 2002." U.S. Census 2003 National Population Estimates, Adults Age 20 and older.

ing to his Spiderman-theme room littered with dozens of swimming ribbons and pentathlon trophies, his mother Stephanie says: "I mean, this kid's active."

In January, Mrs. Holwell noticed a fitness assessment at the bottom of his nearly straight-A report card. Jeremy placed in the 97th national percentile: "overweight," according to the report. She asked the principal to stop including the information on Jeremy's report card, which he agreed to do.

Obesity Battle Traps Obese Parents

Sue Harter, the district's director of food service, says the strictures are becoming overly specific. Snacks sold during the school day can contain no more than seven grams of fat, no more than two grams of saturated fat, and no more than 15 grams of sugar, with a few exceptions. That means no french fries, Tater Tots or Twinkies. Ms. Harter was fine with that, but has balked at a proposal to take away other offerings, including beef jerky and baked chips. "I feel that kids junior high and up should be able to make choices," she says.

Talking about the district's campaign is hard for Ms. Harter. "I was a chunky kid. I've always struggled with my weight," she says, tears welling up. "Here I am, the director of food service, and I'm overweight." Because [of] the new focus on faculty health, "it gives you a feeling of insecurity," she says.

Dr. Fall says that beyond a few negative comments, he doesn't think there has been much public opposition. In any case, the importance of the program "outweighs any temporary hurt feelings," he says. "The kids know they're overweight! They don't want to be overweight! They don't want to be unhappy."

This school year, Dr. Fall intensified his efforts. By December 2006, 171 parents of children in grades three through six had received a letter offering a children's health evaluation and a related fitness program.

Mike Miller, a physical-education teacher hired to run the Healthy Schools initiatives, asked PE teachers to recommend students who might benefit from the program, which would be held after school.

Jim Coca, a physical-education instructor at Wagonwheel Elementary, says he reluctantly gave about 20 names to Mr. Miller, based on the kids with the lowest fitness scores. "I would have rather seen all the kids get a letter," he says. "Make it available to everyone, and you've hurt nobody."

A fifth-grade girl approached Mr. Coca after noticing the letter, addressed to her parents, on the kitchen table. "Mr. Coca, do you think I'm fat?" he recalls her asking. "I knew it hurt our relationship a little bit. She had never thought that she was heavy." Next year, Mr. Coca says, he won't give names. He'll send the fitness data to Mr. Miller and ask him to pick.

Mr. Miller says the PE teachers "would be the better ones to assess kids," but he says he'll use the raw data if necessary. "It will be obvious to us from the BMI and fitness scores if the kid's at risk."

Strong Kids Club Attracts Few

Of nearly 200 letters that went out to families, only 23 parents made an appointment. They were invited to a "Strong Kids Club" exercise group that meets after school at a local recreation center three times a week. Erin Wiley, the assessment program's coordinator, is an enthusiastic, ponytailed 24-year-old who leads third to sixth graders in an hour of exercises. On a recent Tuesday, after teaching eight kids a leg exercise using resistance cords, she wound down the session with a series of yoga poses named after animals—cobra, swan, downward dog, cat and cow.

"How much more of these are we going to do?" whined seven-year-old Ryan Quintana, a second-grader from Pronghorn Elementary School who suffers from asthma.

"It's a whole series!" said Ms. Wiley. "Want to see 'volcano'?"

Many of the families say the assessments and classes —which are free—have helped their kids.

Ryan, for example, was always bigger than his peers in his class, but seemed unaware of it until recently. "I noticed him saying, 'This shirt makes my belly look big' while getting dressed," says his mother, Jaime. "We realized he needs to lose weight."

He has been attending classes three times a week since the fall. He used to dread gym. Now, says his father, Robert, "he talks about how fast he was. I don't think he's Flash Gordon by any means, but he's come a long way."

By the time of his follow-up assessment, Ryan had grown an inch, to 4 feet 6 inches, and had lost two pounds, to 104. He went from a high "body composition," a measure of body fat, to average. His fitness level rose from "fair" to "average."

Before, PE class was "too hard for me," Ryan says. "I had to take my inhaler." Now, he says, it is "not so scary."

Faith Rudland is a 10-year-old fifth-grader at Conestoga Elementary who also attends the fitness classes. When her mother, Heather, received the invitation letter, she was relieved to be getting some help.

"It's not like I'm blind," Mrs. Rudland says. The family had sought the advice of doctors and dieticians to bring down Faith's weight, but nothing worked. One said to watch sodium intake. Another said she would grow into her weight.

When Faith started the Strong Kids Club, she weighed 163 pounds. Now she weighs 145. "It's a learning process for me, too," says Mrs. Rudland, who has cut back on Hamburger Helper and now stocks the fridge with fruit and vegetables.

Faith says the classes "make my life a lot better." She now doesn't get as winded when she runs and earns higher marks in PE.

Obesity Program Is Meddlesome to Some

For other families, the program is an unwelcome intrusion. Brittany Burns "has been a big kid since she was little," says Mrs. Story, her mother. "We're a big-boned family, as is a lot of Wyoming. It's a meat and potatoes state," she says.

Later, she prepares a dinner of exactly that when her husband and brother-in-law come home from the mines, their faces and hands black with grime.

Mrs. Story says that when the letter came, she decided to give the program a chance. She took her daughter, who attends Lakeview Elementary, to an assessment. Brittany started writing down what she ate. By the end of the week, her enthusiasm flagged. She never went back for a follow-up.

"I didn't push the issue," says Mrs. Story. "I didn't want her to think I saw her the same way these people saw her."

> **FAST FACT**
>
> Children who are five to six years old gain more weight in the summer than they do in the entire school year.

High Fructose Corn Syrup Causes Obesity

Kim Severson

Kim Severson, a staff writer with the *San Francisco Chronicle*, presents the case that high fructose corn syrup may be responsible for obesity. Food companies use high fructose corn syrup because it is cheaper than sugar, mixes easily with other food ingredients, extends the shelf life of products, and helps prevent freezer burn. Our bodies do not process this sweetener in the same way they digest cane and beet sugar, according to the author.

An overweight America may be fixated on fat and obsessed with carbs, but nutritionists say the real problem is much sweeter—we're awash in sugar. Not just any sugar, but high fructose corn syrup.

The country eats more sweetener made from corn than from sugarcane or beets, gulping it down in drinks

SOURCE: Kim Severson, "Sugar Coated: We're Drowning in High Fructose Corn Syrup. Do the Risks Go Beyond Our Waistlines?" *San Francisco Chronicle*, February 18, 2004, p. E-1. Republished with permission of *San Francisco Chronicle*, conveyed through Copyright Clearance Center, Inc.

as well as in frozen food and baked goods. Even ketchup is laced with it.

Almost all nutritionists finger high fructose corn syrup consumption as a major culprit in the nation's obesity crisis. The inexpensive sweetener flooded the American food supply in the early 1980s, just about the time the nation's obesity rate started its unprecedented climb.

The question is why did it make us so fat. Is it simply the Big Gulp syndrome—that we're eating too many empty calories in ever-increasing portion sizes? Or does the fructose in all that corn syrup do something more insidious—literally short-wire our metabolism and force us to gain weight?

The debate can divide a group of nutritional researchers almost as fast as whether the low-carb craze is fact or fad.

High Fructose Corn Syrup Is in Many Products

Loading high fructose corn syrup into increasingly larger portions of soda and processed food has packed more calories into us and more money into food processing companies, say nutritionists and food activists. But some health experts argue that the issue is bigger than mere calories. The theory goes like this: The body processes the fructose in high fructose corn syrup differently than it does old-fashioned cane or beet sugar, which in turn alters the way metabolic-regulating hormones function. It also forces the liver to kick more fat out into the bloodstream.

The end result is that our bodies are essentially tricked into wanting to eat more and at the same time, we are storing more fat.

"One of the issues is the ease with which you can consume this stuff," says Carol Porter, director of nutrition and food services at UC San Francisco. "It's not that fructose itself is so bad, but they put it in so much food that you consume so much of it without knowing it."

A single 12-ounce can of soda has as much as 13 teaspoons of sugar in the form of high fructose corn syrup. And because the amount of soda we drink has more than doubled since 1970 to about 56 gallons per person a year, so has the amount of high fructose corn syrup we take in. In 2001, we consumed almost 63 pounds of it, according to the U.S. Department of Agriculture [USDA].

Americans Consume Too Much Sugar

The USDA suggests most of us limit our intake of added sugar—that's everything from the high fructose corn syrup hidden in your breakfast cereal to the sugar cube you drop into your after-dinner espresso—to about 10 to 12 teaspoons a day. But we're not doing so well. In 2000, we ate an average of 31 teaspoons a day, which was more than 15 percent of our caloric intake. And much of that was in sweetened drinks.

So, the answer is to just avoid soda, right? Unfortunately, it's not that simple, because the inexpensive, versatile sweetener has crept into plenty of other places —foods you might not expect to have any at all. A low-fat, fruit-flavored yogurt, for example, can have 10 teaspoons of fructose-based sweetener in one serving.

Because high fructose corn syrup mixes easily, extends shelf-life and is as much as 20 percent cheaper than other sources of sugar, large-scale food manufacturers love it. It can help prevent freezer burn, so you'll find it on the labels of many frozen foods. It helps breads brown and keeps them soft, which is why hot dog buns and even English muffins hold unexpected amounts.

Is High Fructose Corn Syrup a Bad Product?

The question remains just how much more dangerous high fructose corn syrup is than other sugars.

Fructose, as the name implies, is the sugar found naturally in fruit. It can be extracted, turned into granules and used like sugar in the kitchen. It used to be considered a healthier alternative to sucrose—plain old table sugar. It's sweeter, so less is needed to achieve the same taste. Diabetics use it because fructose doesn't stimulate insulin production, so blood sugar levels remain stable.

The process of pulling sugar from cornstarch wasn't perfected until the early 1970s, when Japanese researchers developed a reliable way to turn cornstarch into syrup sweet enough to compete with liquid sugar. After some

Candy made from high fructose corn syrup has been widely touted as a major contributor to the obesity epidemic. (AP Images)

tinkering, they landed on a formula that was 55 percent fructose and 45 percent glucose—sweet enough and cheap enough to make most soda companies jump from liquid sugar to high fructose corn syrup by the 1980s.

The results were dramatic—a whopping increase of 4,080 percent.

Journalist Greg Critser lays out a compelling case against high fructose corn syrup in his 2003 book, *Fat Land: How Americans Became the Fattest People in the World.* He argues that federal policies that aimed to stabilize food prices and support corn production in the 1970s led to a glut of corn and then to high fructose corn syrup. With a cheaper way to sweeten food, producers pumped up the size and amount of sweet snacks and drinks on the market and increased profits.

Obesity and High Fructose Corn Syrup Use Are Correlated

Critser writes that despite the food industry's arguments that sugar is sugar, whether fructose or sucrose, no group "has yet refuted the growing scientific concern that, when all is said and done, fructose . . . is about the furthest thing from natural that one can imagine, let alone eat."

Although some researchers have long been suspicious that too much fructose can cause problems, the latest case against high fructose corn syrup began in earnest a few years ago. Dr. George Bray, principal investigator of the Diabetes Prevention Program at Louisiana State University Medical Center told the International Congress on Obesity that in 1980, just after high fructose corn syrup was introduced in mass quantities, relatively stable obesity rates began to climb. By 2000, they had doubled.

Further, the *American Journal of Clinical Nutrition* in 2002 published research that showed that teenagers' milk consumption between 1965 and 1996 decreased by 36 percent, while soda consumption increased by more than

200 percent. Bray argues that without calcium, which nutritionists agree can help the body regulate weight, kids got fatter. He says that he could find no other single combination of environmental or food changes that were as significant to the rise in obesity.

We Digest Fructose Differently than Glucose

Other studies by researchers at UC Davis and the University of Michigan have shown that consuming fructose, which is more readily converted to fat by the liver, increases the levels of fat in the bloodstream in the form of triglycerides.

And unlike other types of carbohydrate made up of glucose, fructose does not stimulate the pancreas to produce insulin. Peter Havel, a nutrition researcher at UC Davis who studies the metabolic effects of fructose, has also shown that fructose fails to increase the production of leptin, a hormone produced by the body's fat cells.

Both insulin and leptin act as signals to the brain to turn down the appetite and control body weight. And in another metabolic twist, Havel's research shows that fructose does not appear to suppress the production of ghrelin, a hormone that increases hunger and appetite.

> **FAST FACT**
>
> Each year 280,000 people die from the complications of obesity.

"Because fructose in isolation doesn't activate the hormones that regulate body weight as do other types of carbohydrate composed of glucose, consuming a diet high in fructose could lead to taking in more calories and, over time, to weight gain," he says.

However, Havel isn't convinced high fructose corn syrup is by itself the problem. That's in part because it is composed of 55 percent fructose and 45 percent glucose, which is similar to the 50-50 combination of fructose and glucose found in table sugar. Havel's studies have focused

Obesity and High Fructose Corn Syrup

The number of Americans who are obese has quadrupled in recent years, a study shows. At the same time, high fructose corn syrup consumption has risen at parallel rates.

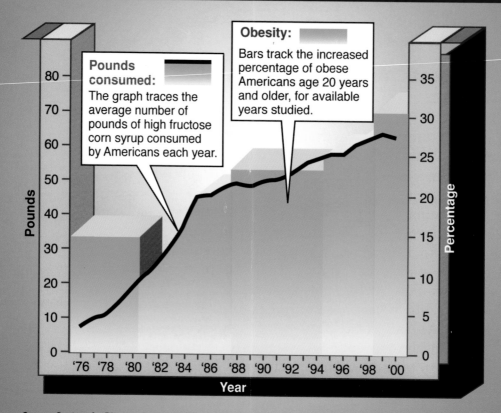

Pounds consumed:
The graph traces the average number of pounds of high fructose corn syrup consumed by Americans each year.

Obesity:
Bars track the increased percentage of obese Americans age 20 years and older, for available years studied.

Source: Centers for Disease Control, American Obesity Association. *San Francisco Chronicle* graphic.

on fructose by itself and not as part of a high fructose corn syrup mixture.

"Whether there is an important difference in the effects of consuming beverages sweetened with a mixture of 55 percent as opposed to 50 percent fructose would be hard to measure," he says. "Additional studies are needed to better understand the nutritional impact of consuming different types of sugars in humans."

Still, other researchers are finding new problems with high fructose corn syrup. A study in last month's [January 2004] *Journal of the National Cancer Institute* suggests that women whose diet was high in total carbohydrate and fructose intake had an increased risk of colorectal cancer. And Dr. Mel Heyman, chief of pediatric gastroenterology and nutrition at UCSF, is seeing sick children whose bodies have been overloaded with fructose from naturally occurring fructose in fruit juice combined with soda and processed food.

"The way the body handles glucose is different than fructose," he says. "It can overload the intestines' ability to absorb carbohydrate by giving it too much fructose. That can cause cramps, bloating and loose stools."

Some Experts Say the Problem Is Just Overeating

Like others in the field, he says there is much to discover in how sugar works, but he disagrees that high fructose corn syrup is somehow reprogramming our bodies toward obesity. Rather, he says, we're just eating too much of it.

Nutrition theory holds that the basic make-up of fructose-laced corn syrup is not much different than table sugar. They react about the same in the body, says Dr. Walter Willett, a professor of epidemiology and nutrition at Harvard School of Public Health. "There are some modest differences in metabolism, but I don't think fructose per se is the culprit."

Neither do the food companies that use it in copious amounts.

Says Stephanie Childs, a spokesperson for the Grocery Manufacturers Association: "At the end of the day, how any sweetener affects your weight depends on how many calories you are taking in overall. Overemphasizing one nutrient at the detriment of others is not going to solve the problem."

Even some leading nutrition reformers aren't convinced that high fructose corn syrup is of itself the issue.

The bigger battle, says Michael Jacobson, executive director of the Center for Science in the Public Interest, a consumer advocacy group, is to get added sugars listed on food labels with a percentage of daily value. That means a consumer could look at a package and see that, for example, one soda provides almost all the sugar a person should eat in a day.

"It simply comes down to this," he says. "We're eating too much refined sugars, be it sucrose or high fructose corn syrup or any other refined sugar."

High Fructose Corn Syrup Does Not Cause Obesity

John S. White and John P. Foreyt

John S. White, president of White Technical Research, and John P. Foreyt, a professor of medicine at Baylor College of Medicine, argue that high fructose corn syrup is not to blame for the obesity crisis. They make the case that obesity is the result of numerous factors and that it is wrong to single out one food ingredient as the cause for this national crisis. The authors note that obesity rates are rising in parts of the world that do not use high fructose corn syrup. They also suggest that tests showing that high fructose corn syrup is digested differently from other sugars were improperly conducted.

High-fructose corn syrup [HFCS], the sweetener used in most carbonated beverages in the United States, drew very little attention over its 30-year history until the past two years, when some researchers in the nutrition community claimed that it bears a unique responsibility for the current obesity epidemic.

SOURCE: John S. White and John P. Foreyt, "Ten Myths About High-Fructose Corn Syrup," *Food Technology*, vol. 60, October 2006, p. 96. Reproduced by permission.

Such claims are largely myths based on misunderstandings of the chemistry, food science, and nutrition of HFCS.

The name high-fructose corn syrup was given to acknowledge its fructose content and to differentiate it from regular corn syrup, which contains only glucose and glucose polymers. HFCS is nearly identical in fructose-to-glucose ratio to sucrose and honey, which explains its comparable metabolism and sweetness.

They are different products, with distinct physical, functional, and metabolic properties. Commercial fructose is pure crystalline fructose. Corn syrup contains only glucose and glucose polymers. HFCS contains nearly equal amounts of fructose and glucose.

HFCS accounts for only about 10% of the world's sweeteners. Since many parts of the world are seeing rising rates of obesity and diabetes despite having little or no HFCS in their foods and beverages, HFCS clearly cannot play a unique role in obesity and diabetes.

HFCS, sugar, and honey are composed of nearly equal amounts of fructose and glucose. Though the absorption of HFCS and honey differs somewhat from that of sucrose, the human body cannot distinguish these sweeteners from one another once they reach the bloodstream. That fructose and glucose have distinct metabolic pathways is unimportant when comparing HFCS, sucrose, and honey, since they all feed the same sugars at the same ratios into the same metabolic pathways.

The supposition that HFCS blocks the body's ability to know when it is full is based on improper extrapolation of data gathered with pure fructose—not a suitable model for HFCS—at exaggerated dietary levels. Recent research directly comparing HFCS to sucrose—a far better model—shows no difference on appetite or satiety [a feeling of fullness] control hormones.

HFCS is made from corn, a natural grain. The process begins by steeping corn to soften and separate

Popular Sweeteners

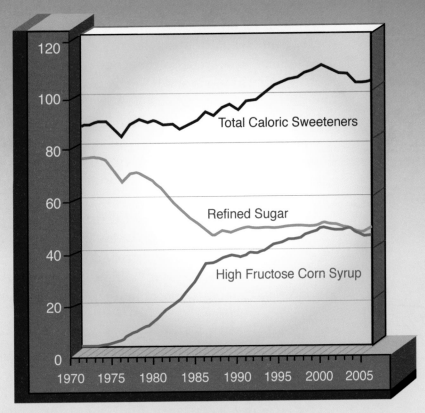

Per Capita Consumption (pounds) of Selected Sweeteners, 1970–2005.

Source: USDA Econ Research Service, *Sugar and Sweetener Yearbook* series, Tables 50–53.

the kernel into its starch, corn hull, protein, and oil components. Many of the subsequent processes used to make HFCS are also used to produce other foods and ingredients that are considered natural. HFCS contains no artificial or synthetic materials or color additives and meets Food and Drug Administration guidelines for natural food ingredients.

Absolutely no data support this notion. Both ingredients have received the same clean bill of health from every expert body that has evaluated their impact on human health.

Those claiming this and implying that this has seduced the public into consuming greater quantities of foods have misreported the literature on sweetness. HFCS-55 was intentionally designed to be equal in sweetness to sucrose so that they could be used interchangeably in foods and beverages.

Price may have catalyzed the switch from sucrose to HFCS 20 years ago, but its unique functional properties have sustained its use. It benefits consumers by reducing food spoilage, retaining moisture in foods, helping canned foods taste fresher, enhancing fruit and spice flavors, and prolonging shelf life. Food companies value its ease of use in liquid formulations and its stability in acidic products, providing superior performance in carbonated beverages and fruit preparations.

> **FAST FACT**
>
> The single biggest factor in the onset of type 2 diabetes is obesity.

While the U.S. government provides support to certain farmers to guarantee a stable farm economy and a reliable food supply, manufacturers of HFCS do not receive these subsidies.

Corn used to produce HFCS may or may not come from genetically enhanced grain. However, corn DNA is removed during processing and cannot be detected in measurable amounts in HFCS.

In summary, HFCS—like other carbohydrates, fats, proteins, and alcohol—is a caloric ingredient. If foods and beverages containing any ingredient are overconsumed, weight gain will likely occur.

Obesity is a complex problem. Attacking a single ingredient as the sole cause is clearly wrong and counterproductive, because it stands in the way of our finding true and effective solutions.

rsonal Perspectives on Obesity

One Patient Describes Gastric Bypass Surgery

Melisa McNulty

Melisa McNulty recounts her experience in coping with obesity and the lengths to which she went to solve her weight problem. At age sixteen she weighed three hundred pounds and was the subject of ridicule. Melisa elected to undergo gastric bypass surgery, a procedure that stapled off part of her stomach to limit the amount of food she could eat. She explains how the medical screening process works to determine whether a person is eligible for this extreme solution. She describes her feelings both before and after the surgery, how she adapted to her new dietary restrictions, and how it felt to buy new clothes after losing one hundred pounds in a year.

Photo on previous page. Journal keeping can be a tool in combating problems such as obesity. **(AP Images)**

I've always been fat. I can say it, because it's a fact: I inherited genetic obesity from my dad's side of my family and have been severely overweight since the age of two. By the time I turned 16, I weighed 300 pounds and could barely fit into the desks at school. In

SOURCE: Melisa McNulty, "I Had My Stomach Stapled," *Teen People,* vol. 5, November 1, 2002, p. 118. Copyright © 2002 Melisa McNulty. Reproduced by permission of the author.

elementary school I was called names, like "Free Willy." In middle school, people would look at me and whisper. Or I'd tell my best friend that I liked a guy and somehow he'd always find out and be really mean to me, as if I'd done something wrong. I also faced major medical risks—practically all of my dad's relatives have problems with diabetes and heart disease. I tried dieting and working out, but it was discouraging; I'd work so hard and wouldn't see any results. That's why when I heard about gastric bypass surgery (GBS), a procedure in which your stomach is stapled to help you eat less food, I decided to try it. Some people may think it's drastic, but to me, it felt like my only hope.

Gastric Bypass Surgery Offers Hope

06.03.01 I first heard about GBS about two weeks ago, when my mom told me that a woman at her work had had it done. My mom thought the operation might be an option for me. I've found out the surgery works like this: My stomach would be stapled off and divided into a very small upper pouch (about the size of a man's thumb) and a larger lower part. The lower part would remain functional but no longer receive any food. Meanwhile, my small intestine would be shortened and connected directly to the little part of the stomach that holds food. That way, I'll feel satisfied after eating only a little bit. When my stomach heals, I'll be able to eat almost any kind of food I want—only in very tiny (about half-cup) portions. It's a major deal: The operation is permanent, so I'll have to stick to a strict diet the rest of my life. But it still sounds worth it.

08.12.01 I'm using the same doctor as my mom's friend. Today I spent the entire day in what's called the "interview process" to determine if I'm eligible for the surgery. I met with nurses, nurse practitioners and other staff members about my medical history, was given physical exams and finally met with my doctor. Basically, he wanted to make sure I was mature enough for the responsibilities that come after the operation, like the diet and having to take vitamins every day. We talked about what I wanted—not to be tiny, like a supermodel, but just do what my friends do—and about the risks. In the end, I was approved.

09.14.01 I finally got scheduled for surgery; it's tomorrow. I spent most of today—from eight in the morning until three this afternoon—in the hospital doing prep stuff. Then they sent me home with a special drink that was basically a big laxative and told me not to eat anything. I've spent pretty much the whole evening on the toilet. I'm not feeling so hot physically, but emotionally I'm really excited.

09.15.0.1 I woke up at 3 A.M. so I could be at the hospital for my 5 a.m. surgery. I took a shower, got dressed in loose-fitting clothes and packed a bag, since I'll be staying for three days. Right before we got in the car, my mom took a "before" photo of me.

Recovery from Surgery Is No Fun

I don't remember much after I was wheeled into preop. The doctor came in and asked if I was nervous, then started the anesthetic, and that was it. When I woke up three or four hours later, I had a tube in my throat, making me gag. I could hear the nurses telling me that I needed to keep the tube down to help me breathe. They asked if I wanted my mom to come in and I shook my head no; I didn't want her to see me like that. A few hours later, they returned me to my room.

09.16.01 It's the next day, and I feel really uncomfortable. I have six one-inch incisions in my abdomen, and the entire area is swollen. I'm still on major painkillers, so it feels both numb and achy. I can barely move. This morning the nurses gave me some ice chips and then a bit of water, and later on I had the tiniest bit of chicken broth and Jell-O. That's all I'll be able to eat for the next two weeks. One more day here, and then I go home.

09.30.01 It's been a couple of weeks since the surgery, and today was my first day back at school. It was good to see my friends and do something besides lie around, So far, I haven't really lost much weight, so the only thing that's different is the food I eat. I can have scrambled eggs now—not a huge improvement, but it's

Cutting your hunger

Gastric bypass surgery is effective for helping appropriate patients achieve significant weight loss. The Roux-en-Y procedure is one of several variations of the surgery, which is raising concerns about serious risks.

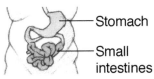

Stomach

Small intestines

An estimated 110,000 people will have gastric bypass surgery this year, 85 percent will be women.

20% may have complications

0.5% to 2% may be fatal

	Step one	**Step two**
Procedure	Reduce stomach size	Curtail calorie absorption
	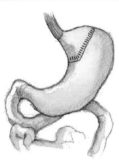 The stomach is divided with staples into a small, upper part (through which food will pass) and a large, lower part.	A portion of the small intestines is attached to the small, upper part of the stomach so that food bypasses the large, lower part. 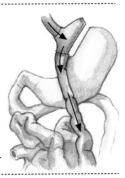
Intended result	Person feels full faster because there is less room for food.	Less calories are absorbed because parts of stomach and small intestines are bypassed.

Source: National Institutes of Health. **(AP Images)**

something. Next week I'm supposed to add yogurt and peanut butter, then harder foods like chicken and beans.

11.01.01 Last night, when we were handing out treats for Halloween, I ate a "fun-size" candy bar and got sweaty and shaky, like I was going to faint. My body couldn't handle the sugar. If you eat sweets, you're supposed to have them with a meal, and I ate the chocolate a couple of hours after dinner. It was so scary, I don't want candy anymore.

Surgery Brings Noticeable Results

12.05.01 Today I finally told my mom I needed to get some new clothes. We were trying to wait because we knew I'd be going through a lot of size changes, but I'm at the point where I can't even hold my pants up with a belt—I'm four sizes smaller than I used to be. One thing makes me sad: My mom says she notices my weight loss, but most of my friends don't talk about it with me. I think it makes them uncomfortable. I wish they would compliment me; it's really motivating.

01.25.02 I've lost about 80 pounds. It's amazing. I still crave carbs, like spaghetti and pizza, which I have to limit, but I can have pretty much anything else. I've always loved food, but I used to use it to help me feel better when I was upset. When I was full, I felt comforted, at least for the time being. Now, that's not an option: If I overeat, I'll throw up or feel sick for hours. The weirdest thing is the excess skin hanging on my arms and stomach. My doctor explained that skin has a six-month delay before it will adjust to my new size. The weight training I plan to start will speed it up.

03.22.02 It's almost a year since I first heard about the surgery, and I weigh 200 pounds, which means I've lost about 100—and I'm still losing. I'll stop eventually when my stomach adapts. My goal is 150 pounds. The other day I went into Old Navy and bought a pair of regular-size pants. To everyone else, it's no big deal, but for me, it's huge. Before I'd just stay home and watch TV, but now I get out and do things. My family and I will take our dogs to a field near our house and I'll run around with them. I also look in the mirror a lot now because I feel more attractive. I even got my lip pierced! It's something I always wanted to do, but I never would have done it before, because I thought people would make fun of me. I'm definitely looking forward to dating guys too. I'm more confident around them now, maybe even a little flirty. After 16 years, I finally feel like myself.

Metabolic Change Can Cause Obesity

The Endocrine Society

Sometimes weight gain is not caused by overeating and lack of exercise. This article tells the story of nine-year-old Donna Marie Bloomquest whose weight gain came quite suddenly. Medical exam-inations revealed that Donna Marie had developed type 2 diabetes, a metabolic condition, and hypothyroidism. The article tells how she entered into a twelve-week weight-loss program with nutritionists, psychologists, and endocrinologists to customize a program for her. The lifestyle changes to control weight and thyroid disease affect the entire family, but they can be managed. Donna Marie's mother rec-ommends that parents should seek the help of an endocrinologist if their children experience sudden weight gain.

The Endocrine Society is an international organization that seeks to educate the general population, as well as medical professionals, about endocrinology.

Approximately three years ago, nine-year-old Donna Marie Bloomquest began to gain weight unexplainably. Not an overeater or one to be

SOURCE: The Endocrine Society, "Profiles in Obesity." http://obesity inamerica.org. Reproduced by permission.

sedentary, Donna Marie's body was suddenly changing for no apparent reason. She was embarrassed, confused and fearful that she had done something wrong to cause this change. Within one year, she had gained an astonishing 20 pounds.

Her mother, Christine, became very concerned about Donna Marie's weight gain, turning to her daughter's pediatrician for answers. Unfortunately, Donna Marie's pediatrician did not diagnose her condition as a characteristic of metabolic syndrome and the youngster's weight continued to climb.

Endocrinologist Diagnoses the Problems

A referral from a friend resulted in both mother and daughter visiting with a specialist—an endocrinologist named Dr. Henry Anhalt. Dr. Anhalt's "Kids Weight-Down" program is a program that caters to the specific needs of overweight children, childhood (pediatric) obesity, and their families. Designed to address all elements of a person's weight loss—overall health, diet, lifestyle, etc.—this 12-week-long program incorporates the input from nutritionists and psychologists as well an endocrine team to customize each child's program.

At the first appointment, Dr. Anhalt noticed a ring around the back of Donna Marie's neck—a tell-[tale] sign that she had severe insulin resistance—and quickly diagnosed her with Type 2 diabetes, dyslipidemia (elements of the metabolic syndrome) and hypothyroidism. Donna Marie weighed 140 pounds.

In addition to a regimen of Metformin® twice a day and obesity medications designed to reduce her lipid levels and treat Donna Marie's thyroid disease, hypothyroidism, she actively participated in Dr. Anhalt's "Kids Weight-Down" program for weight loss. With her mother's support, Donna Marie met with behavioral therapists and nutritionists who assessed her childhood

Watching too much television can lead to a slowing metabolic rate. (AP Images)

(pediatric) obesity situation, identified reachable goals and developed a customized weight loss program.

Weight Loss Program Brings Changes for Family

Donna Marie emerged from the weight loss program with stronger eating and living habits, and has been able to wrangle her blood sugar to normal levels (without needing insulin typically needed with diabetes), while getting her lipid and thyroid hormone levels under control. Despite Donna's improved health profile now, she currently weighs 180 pounds and continues to gain weight—an issue being addressed by Dr. Anhalt and his team during Donna's monthly check-in appointments.

Her mother says that while the teasing Donna Marie experiences at school hurts her, the youngster is determined to be successful in weight loss and is very receptive to treatment—she even asked her mother for a treadmill for Christmas.

The changes in Donna Marie's life to cope with her thyroid disease (hypothyroidism) and related childhood (pediatric) obesity issues are not easy and require lifestyle modifications by the whole family. Christine is a vegetarian who lives for carbohydrates—mostly pasta and bread. Now, she has to sneak them. But Christine is grateful that her daughter is learning how to manage her thyroid disease (hypothyroidism) condition rather than risk developing an eating disorder down the road as a remedy to her weight loss issue.

Lifestyle Changes Must Be Lifelong

"In order for a patient to really benefit long-term from obesity treatment, they need lifelong support systems in place," says Dr. Anhalt. "Most patients, especially children, need reinforcement to maintain the lifestyle changes necessary to regain what's been lost as a result of obesity. Each child should be treated based on their own unique needs."

> **FAST FACT**
>
> Worldwide 20 million children are overweight.

Christine, a single mom, recommends that any mother who sees changes in their children's weight should immediately seek out the care of an endocrinologist. She says that her daughter's pediatrician was a barrier to Donna Marie's hypothyroidism diagnosis and, she feels, may have actually cost her valuable treatment time.

Christine wants people to think about obesity and its causes before they judge the way others look. Acknowledging the looks people give her daughter, she challenges others to consider the possibility that people may be obese because of a medical condition (like thyroid disease, hypothyroidism), not just because they "sit at home and stuff their faces."

Donna Marie's health and childhood (pediatric) obesity issues are slowly improving and she hopes to get back to looking "normal." Although she faces a lifetime of obesity medication, especially for her thyroid disease (hypothyroidism) condition, Donna Marie continues to fight childhood (pediatric) obesity, maintaining a positive outlook and remaining vigilant in her weight loss and treatment.

A Daughter's Painful Realization

Elizabeth Daley

Elizabeth Daley has her PhD in communication. She is a writer and mother of two. In this narrative Daley discusses a period of emotional growth in her young daughter's life. At school her daughter Emily is called fat and encouraged to recognize how her weight separates her from the rest of the kids her age. Daley attempts to dismiss these ideas so that Emily will not be affected by society's value of outer beauty. When Emily cannot avoid the social burden of her body, an intergenerational struggle is revealed between Emily and her mother.

Emily was articulate and tall for her age, a sturdy girl by any measure. On stout little legs she participated fully in her world. She sang with gusto in the children's chorus at the university. She volunteered to perform in junior drama classes at the local rec center, while the other children hung back. She taught herself to read and write, asking hungry questions about words in

SOURCE: Elizabeth Daley, "Sturdy Girl," *Mothering*. Reproduced by permission.

books, on signs, in the grocery store. Perched in her car seat, she rode around town expectantly, as if any moment might hold the seed of her next adventure.

Friends came easily to Emily, perhaps attracted by the confidence she carried. The antics of her silliest playmates were rewarded with a full-bodied laugh, while more sensitive companions could count on her sympathy. Once, at her preschool, she was found comforting an upset child who was characterized by their teacher as "unapproachable." Though the child hated to have anyone touch her, the two were seen sitting next to each other in the art room, Emily's arm slung around the child's shoulder, whispering in her ear.

Emily was big-boned, larger than her peers. In those carefree preschool years, she moved among her many friends with a blessed lack of self-consciousness; but by kindergarten her blithe spirit had begun to wilt, poisoned by the notion that there might be something different and unacceptable about her. Her transformation began with a single word: fat.

The Dreaded Day

I remember clearly the day she mentioned an incident that had taken place on the playground. We were ambling to the car in the shade of a massive live oak, a cool breeze muting the heat of the late spring sun. My mind was busy with everyday concerns—groceries to buy, unanswered phone messages, the checking account balance. Suddenly Emily's sweet voice interrupted my mundane reverie. "Mama," she said, "do you think I'm fat?"

I stopped as if the ground before me had fallen away. My mind raced, anxiously sifting through five years of parenting advice from friends, books, magazines, and assorted strangers. I sought a reply that would obliterate the very word and all its connotations from Emily's consciousness. Turning to squat face to face, I looked directly into her eyes. "No, you're not fat," I said firmly, pulling her close to testify softly in her ear. "You're perfect," I whispered. "You're perfect just the way you are."

Emily put her arms around my neck, and I hoisted her to my hip. As I carried her to the car she pressed her cheek against mine. "Matthew said I was fat," she confided as she climbed into her car seat. Heat shot into my head and throat; a deep instinct to protect Emily from a pain I knew too well had been aroused. I could feel the spirit of Mother Superior, the holy terror of my parochial school days, rising in me. Stifling an urge to condemn the character of a five-year-old boy, I kissed Emily's forehead, offering quick assurances.

"Everyone is beautiful in a different way," I said carefully. "You're the best you there is, you know." Before I shut the car door, I looked into Emily's eyes and was relieved to see neither suspicion nor history there—no memories of teasing by family members, of dreadful summers around lean bikini-wearers, of the hated euphemism "pleasantly plump." Such were the travails of my life, not hers. I never would have swallowed reassuring platitudes from my mother, who once laughed about my "big behind" (to the delight of my little brother) as I walked from her room. But Emily had every reason to believe me, and she did.

What Emily Needs

Emily trusted me, I think, because I'd always tried to listen to her, carrying the wish to be heard and understood all the way from my own childhood. Infant tears, toddler tantrums, preschool tirades—my husband and I treated them all like vital messages in need of decoding. Rather than cajole or threaten, we'd listen closely and hear "I need sleep" or "I'm overwhelmed" or "I'm afraid." Then we'd understand, and know what she needed from us. Except that this time, I didn't.

For one thing, I was not at all sure that Emily's size was in fact a problem. One hundred years ago, I reasoned, before Twiggy and Kate Moss and Gap ads featuring waif-like children in seductive poses, Emily's hearty body might have been seen as a sign of health and prosperity, not a cause for shame. Still, I had to admit that I'd fretted periodically about her devotion to typical kid foods like macaroni and cheese and ice cream, and compared her solid frame to the willowy five and six year olds at swim lessons. But I'd restricted discussion about her size to quiet, late-night talks with my husband, scrupulously avoiding references to diets or weight problems in Emily's presence.

That night I lay awake considering my options. A strict change in diet might have short-term results but create the conditions for a later eating disorder. I could carp about materialism and the fashion industry—but to a five and a half year old? When asked about Emily's weight at her last checkup, our pediatrician had assured me that she would "grow into her body" in time. So I stuck with the idea that seemed to make the most sense: Offer healthy food, keep Emily active, and simply insist that her body was fine as it was.

Emily's Observation

For the next six months, we lived blissfully free of the topic of weight. Then one day, Emily went to spend the afternoon with her best friend Katie, a petite, elfin child with red hair and perky disposition. At bath time that night, Emily asked me not to look when she took off her clothes. Once submerged she suddenly looked perplexed. "Mama, why do I have such a big belly?" she asked. "Am I fat?" In a flash, I knew that Katie had shared some keen observations with Emily. Without missing a beat I said with conviction, "Honey, you're perfect. You're perfect just the way you are."

And so I embarked on the path of denial and evasion in response to Emily's poignant requests for the truth of who she really was. I didn't want to deceive her. I wanted to convince her of a wholly unpopular notion: that one's physical self was infinitely less important than the depth of one's heart and the breadth of one's mind. I hoped to shield Emily from the tyranny of "lookism" by giving her the same reply each time she asked about her weight: "You know, you are beautiful. Everyone is different. Your body is just right for you."

One night, I had kissed Emily's cheek, whispered a wish for sweet dreams in her ear, and was reaching for the light on her nightstand when she implored, "Mama, I feel so fat." My deep sigh contained a message, and Emily knew it. "I do," she moaned, "I am fat." Mechanically I commenced my reply. "Sweetie, you are not fat." Swiftly, Emily sat up, weeping angrily. "Mama, you aren't listening to me! I know I'm fat! You aren't listening!" I sat down heavily on the bed. She was right.

> **FAST FACT**
>
> If a parent is overweight or obese, a child has an 80 percent chance of becoming overweight as well.

The Moment of Truth

In all other matters, in her greatest disappointments and smallest displeasures, I'd worked hard to validate even the most disagreeable of Emily's feelings. I'd read *How to Talk So Kids Will Listen*, and *How to Listen So Kids Will Talk*, taken parenting classes, and role-played active listening techniques with my husband. I'd breathed through Emily's early outbursts, trying to convey the message that while particular behaviors might be inappropriate at times, all feelings were appropriate all the time, anytime. I'd aspired to be a mother Emily could talk to about anything, so that she'd never have to hide her anger, fear, or sadness. And suddenly I saw clearly the extent to which I'd failed.

All these months I'd assumed that the evil in our midst was this profound and ubiquitous bigotry of body. I'd railed against it and resisted it, and ultimately I had failed to protect Emily from the force of its intolerance by pretending it had no power. I sat on the bed next to Emily, put my head in my hands, and cried. I'd left my beloved little girl alone in the face of an onslaught of image-hype from the covers of magazines at the grocery store, billboards on the highway, and kids at the playground. No wonder she kept asking me to tell her [the] truth.

Emily set her hand on my leg and asked what was wrong. In an instant the wall between us, the accumulation of 43 years of my own fear and self-loathing, disappeared with her touch. I lay next to Emily, her small head resting on my shoulder, and told her a story about a "pleasantly plump" young girl who became a mother and couldn't bear her child's pain. About a mother who held a wish for her daughter's spirit to fly free, unburdened by concerns about her precious little body. I told her I'd been wrong. I asked her what she thought and felt. And then I listened.

GLOSSARY

adipose tissue Fat tissue.

atherosclerosis A narrowing of the blood vessels due to a buildup of fatty deposits, which restricts the flow of blood.

bariatrics The field of medicine that studies obesity and related medical problems.

body mass index (BMI) An index used to measure a person's weight against a standard. Body mass is the measurement of one's weight in relation to one's height. Body mass index over 25 is considered overweight, and body mass index over 30 is considered obese.

catecholamine A chemical in the brain that controls appetite, among other things. Appetite suppressant medicines help elevate the level of this chemical.

cholesterol A waxy substance found in the bloodstream and tissues of the body. When cholesterol is high, some adheres to the sides of the blood vessels. In time cholesterol builds up, causing a narrowing of the arteries that reduces the flow of blood.

coronary heart disease (CHD) Heart disease that is related to a narrowing of the arteries. CHD is the most common cause of sudden death because it can often lead to heart failure.

dietary fiber Includes the plant cell wall, gums, and bran. These plant parts cannot be digested.

gastric bypass surgery The surgical process of making the stomach smaller to limit appetite and rearranging the small intestine so that food passes through only part of it and fewer calories are absorbed. This operation is recommended for chronically obese people.

high fructose corn syrup	A liquid sweetener derived from cornstarch. The sweetener is used in most non-diet sodas and many processed foods.
hyperplastic obesity	Weight gain in childhood. This type of obesity is marked by the creation of new fat cells.
hypertrophic obesity	Weight gain in adulthood. This type of obesity is marked by the expansion of existing fat cells.
ideal weight	The weight corresponding to the lowest death rate for individuals of a specific height, gender, and age.
leptin	A protein hormone that regulates hunger and eating behavior. Obesity may be related to insensitivity to this hormone.
obese	Weighing more than 30 percent over one's ideal weight.
saturated fat	Especially found in meat and dairy products, saturated fats are associated with higher levels of cholesterol and increased risk of heart disease.
sedentary lifestyle	An inactive lifestyle that includes little physical activity. Sedentary lifestyles are a major factor in the rising obesity rates in the United States and other industrialized nations.
serotonin	A chemical in the brain that controls appetite, among other things. Appetite suppressant medicines help elevate the level of this chemical.
trans fat	Produced as a result of hydrogenating naturally occurring fat to further saturate it. For example, vegetable oil is made into margarine by hydrogenation. Trans fats are associated with a higher risk of heart disease.

CHRONOLOGY

1577–1640   Artist Peter Paul Rubens paints plump female figures, marking the high social status of those who could afford to eat well.

1902   The Automat opens in Philadelphia. It is the first fast food restaurant in the United States. The idea spreads to New York City in 1912 and then throughout the country. The restaurants operate into the 1970s.

1963   Weight Watchers is founded by Jean Nidetch. It now has forty-six thousand employees and operates in thirty countries.

1966   Dr. Edward E. Mason of the University of Iowa develops gastric bypass surgery as a weight reduction procedure after studying patients with other types of stomach surgery.

British model Twiggy lands her first modeling contract and becomes a cultural icon for thinness.

1974   Richard Simmons opens his first weight loss and exercise center in Beverly Hills, California. It is still operating there under the name "Slimmons."

1994   Scientists isolate the hormone leptin that regulates hunger and internal weight control.

1995 The American Obesity Association is founded by Richard L. Atkinson, MD, and Judith S. Stern, ScD, RD, to provide research and education about obesity as a disease. It opens its headquarters in Washington, D.C., in 1997.

2002 Trial lawyer Samuel Hirsch files the first of several lawsuits against McDonald's on behalf of obese clients on July 24. The first client is a fifty-six-year old man who weighs 272 pounds. Subsequent clients are obese children.

2003 Judge Thomas Sweet dismisses Hirsch's second lawsuit against McDonald's on September 5.

2005 A federal judge reinstates the McDonald's obesity case on January 25 on a technicality.

2006 Overweight people outnumber malnourished people worldwide, according to the World Health Organization. About 1 billion are overweight, compared to 800 million who are hungry.

Obesity rates rise in thirty-one states.

ORGANIZATIONS TO CONTACT

The editors have compiled the following list of organizations concerned with the issues debated in this book. The descriptions are derived from materials provided by the organizations. All have publications or information available for interested readers. Most of these publications are available online and can be downloaded for free in HTML or PDF format. The list was compiled on the date of publication of the present volume; the information provided here may change. Be aware that many organizations take several weeks or longer to respond to inquiries, so allow as much time as possible.

American Heart Association National Center
7272 Greenville Ave.
Dallas, TX 75231
(800) 242-8721
www.american
heart.org

The American Heart Association is a national voluntary health agency that promotes cardiovascular health. The Web site provides important information on how to recognize signs of heart attack, stroke, and cardiac arrest. Information can also be found about a wider range of diseases and conditions and about smart choices to benefit a healthy lifestyle.

American Obesity Association
1250 24th St.,
Suite 300
Washington,
DC 20037
(202) 776-7711
or (800) 98-OBESE
www.obesity1.temp
domainname.com

The American Obesity Association is the only organization focused on changing public policy and perceptions of obesity. The Web site provides stories of those struggling with obesity, information about govercent tax breaks and disability claims, as well as advice about prevention and treatment.

American Society for Metabolic and Bariatric Surgery
100 SW 75th St., Suite 201
Gainesville, FL 32607
(352) 331-4900
www.asbs.org

The American Society for Metabolic and Bariatric Surgery works to advance bariatric surgery through investigation, idea exchange, and educational programs. The Web site supplies information for patients and health care professionals about bariatric surgery and the society's meetings and classes.

American Society of Bariatric Physicians
2821 S. Parker Rd., Suite 625
Aurora, CO 80014
(877) 266-6834
www.asbp.org

The American Society of Bariatric Physicians is an international association dedicated to maintaining practice guidelines and providing education. The Web site offers information, tips, and references.

International Association for the Study of Obesity
231 N. Gower St.
London NW1 2NR
United Kingdom
www.iaso.org

The International Association for the Study of Obesity includes fifty-two member national obesity associations to represent fifty-six countries in all. The organization works to improve global health, and the Web site connects the public to its members and their conferences and reports.

National Institute of Diabetes and Digestive and Kidney Diseases
Bldg. 31, Rm. 9A06
31 Center Dr., MSC 2560
Bethesda, MD 20892
(301) 496-3583
www.niddk.nih.gov

The National Institute of Diabetes and Digestive and Kidney Diseases conducts and supports research on serious diseases. The Web site has information on research opportunities and the diseases that affect public health.

Obesity Action Coalition
4511 N. Himes Ave., Suite 250
Tampa, FL 33614
(800) 717-3117 or
(813) 872-7835
www.obesityaction.org

The Obesity Action Coalition aims to empower and educate those affected by obesity. The Web site gives opportunities for public advocacy, as well as resources for facts, support, and personal stories.

Obesity Education Initiative
PO Box 30105
Bethesda, MD 20824
(301) 592-8573
www.nhlbi.nih.gov/about/oei

The Obesity Education Initiative was started by the National Heart, Lung, and Blood Institute to reduce the prevalence of overweight and physical inactivity in order to reduce the risk of related health problems. The Web site provides menu planners, a body mass index calculator, and information on portions and healthy choices.

Obesity Society
8630 Fenton St., Suite 918
Silver Spring, MD 20910
(301) 563-6526
www.naaso.org

The Obesity Society leads scientific research to prevent and treat obesity. The society's Web site offers succinct fact sheets, statistics, and guidelines for diagnoses and treatments.

Shape Up America!
www.shapeup.org

Shape Up America! is an organization dedicated to public awareness of what physical activity and food choices mean to healthy body weight. The Web site provides detailed advice for achieving healthy body weight, as well as a contact page for submitting questions to a knowledgeable staff.

FOR FURTHER READING

Books

Frances Berg, *Underage and Overweight: America's Obesity Crisis—What Every Family Needs to Know.* Long Island City, NY: Hatherleigh, 2004.

Paul Campos, *The Obesity Myth.* New York: Gotham, 2004.

Abby Ellin, *Teenage Waistland.* New York: Public Affairs, 2005.

Carol A. Johnson, *Self-Esteem Comes in All Sizes.* New York: Doubleday, 1995.

Francine R. Kaufman, *Diabesity: The Obesity-Diabetes Epidemic That Threatens America—And What We Must Do to Stop It.* New York: Bantam, 2005.

J. Eric Oliver, *Fat Politics: The Real Story Behind America's Obesity Epidemic.* New York: Oxford University Press, 2006.

Sylvia Rimm, *Rescuing the Emotional Lives of Overweight Children: What Our Kids Go Through—And How We Can Help.* Emmaus, PA: Rodale, 2004.

J. Clinton Smith, *Childhood Obesity.* Jackson: University Press of Mississippi, 1999.

Lisa Tertamella, Elaine Herscher, and Chris Woolston, *Generation Extra Large: Rescuing Our Children from the Epidemic of Obesity.* New York: Basic Books, 2004.

Kimberly A. Tessmer, *Conquering Childhood Obesity for Dummies.* New York: Wiley, 2006.

Periodicals

"Bottled Obesity," *New Scientist,* March 17, 2007.

Paul Ernsberger, "Health Benefits of Obesity," *Health at Every Size,* Winter 2007.

Kathryn Foxhall, "Beginning to Begin," *American Journal of Public Health*, December 2006.

W. Wayt Gibbs, "Obesity: An Overblown Epidemic?" *Scientific American Special Edition*, December 2006.

Katherine Hobson, "A Plateful of Myths," *U.S. News & World Report*, January 22, 2007.

James Holt, Larry Warren, and Rick Wallace, "What Behavioral Interventions Are Safe and Effective for Treating Obesity?" *Journal of Family Practice*, June 2006.

Stephen Holt, "Obesity and Longevity," *Total Health*, January/February 2007.

Sheldon H. Jacobson and Laura A. McLay, "The Economic Impact of Obesity on Automobile Fuel Consumption," *Engineering Economist*, 2006.

"Keep Your Weight Normal to Live Longer," *Tufts University Health and Nutrition Letter*, November 2006.

Elaine Khosrova, "Smart Snacks," *Natural Health*, May 2007.

Alison Motluk, "Supersize Surprises," *New Scientist*, November 4, 2006.

David Nayor, "Green Tea: Natural Support for Healthy Weight Control," *Life Extension*, April 2007.

"Overweight at Midlife Linked to Mortality Risk," *PT: Magazine of Physical Therapy*, November 2006.

Laina Shulman, "Is Super Size the New Normal?" *Alive: Canadian Journal of Health and Nutrition*, February 2007.

Marsha D. Simon, "Losing the War on Weight," *Black Enterprise*, May 2007.

"State-Specific Prevalence of Obesity Among Adults—United States, 2005," *Morbidity and Mortality Weekly Report*, September 15, 2006.

Pat Thomas, "A Big Fat Problem," *Ecologist*, December 2006.

Jessica Thoms, "Global Obesity," *Faces*, March 2007.

Dave Tuttle, "New Strategy to Overcome 'Emotional Eating,'" *Life Extension*, April 2, 2007.

Alissa Zuellig, "Obesity," *Hispanic*, June/July 2006.

INDEX